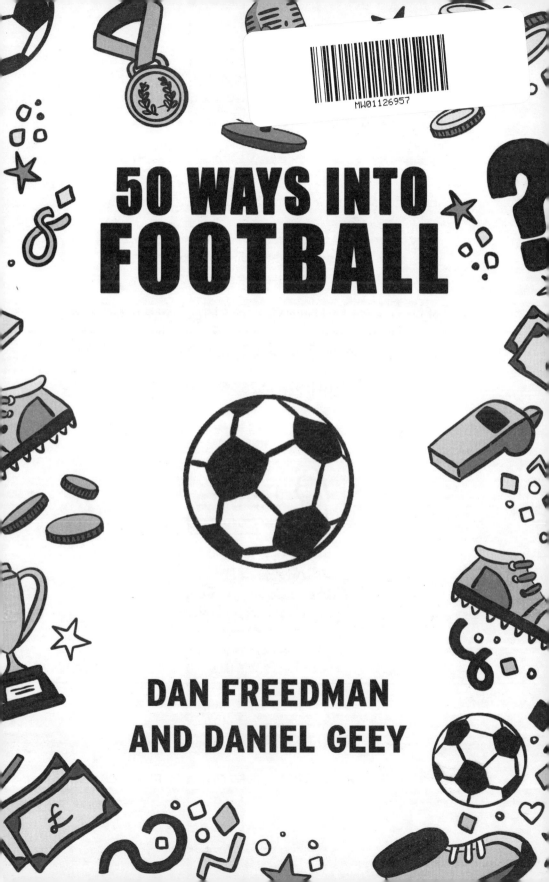

50 WAYS INTO FOOTBALL

DAN FREEDMAN
AND DANIEL GEEY

Thank you to our amazing parents and step-parents, Lillian, Neil, David, Anne, Judy, Ivan and Brian, for the opportunities and support you've given us in pursuing a career in the sport we love.

First published in Great Britain in 2024 by Wren & Rook

ISBN: 978 1 5263 6673 3

1 3 5 7 9 10 8 6 4 2

MIX
Paper | Supporting
responsible forestry
FSC
www.fsc.org
FSC® C104740

Wren & Rook
An imprint of
Hachette Children's Group
Part of Hodder & Stoughton
Carmelite House
50 Victoria Embankment
London EC4Y 0DZ

An Hachette UK Company
www.hachette.co.uk
www.hachettechildrens.co.uk

Printed and bound in Great Britain by Clays Ltd, Elcograf S.p.A.

Foreword by **DECLAN RICE**

50 WAYS INTO
FOOTBALL

DREAM
JOBS
ON AND OFF
THE PITCH

Illustrated by Jorge Garcia

DAN FREEDMAN AND DANIEL GEEY

CONTENTS

TEAM TALK BY DECLAN RICE

INTRODUCTION

PRE-MATCH BUILD-UP

TIPS FROM THE TOP: ADVICE FROM YOUR BIGGEST SUPPORTERS IN THE GAME

KICK-OFF

TIPS FROM THE TOP: ADVICE FROM YOUR BIGGEST SUPPORTERS IN THE GAME

HALF-TIME ENTERTAINMENT

 DECLAN'S GAMEPLAN FOR SUCCESS!
TIPS FROM THE TOP:
ADVICE FROM YOUR BIGGEST
SUPPORTERS IN THE GAME

BACK DOWN TO BUSINESS

 YOUR WAY INTO FOOTBALL : QUIZ

POST-MATCH INTERVIEWS

TEAM TALK BY

Ever since I was young, I have dreamt of becoming a professional footballer. Fortunately for me, that dream became a reality. However, given my love of the game, I know that if I hadn't made it as a football player, as so many people don't, I still would have wanted to have a job in football.

Being a professional footballer, I get to work with a lot of people who have different roles within the game and most of these jobs I wouldn't have known about if I wasn't in the football world. That's why I'm so excited to introduce *50 Ways Into Football* to you.

There are so many exciting jobs within football and this book will tell you all about them and help you discover new ways into your favourite sport. If you love the game like me and want to work in football, then this is the book for you.

DECLAN RICE

Whether it's coaching or analytics or marketing, the variety of jobs in the world of football is bigger than you think, so no matter what you're good at there will be something for you!

Whatever path you decide to take, if you **work hard, believe in yourself** and **don't give up** then you will be successful.

I hope you enjoy reading the book and find your dream job!

Declan Rice

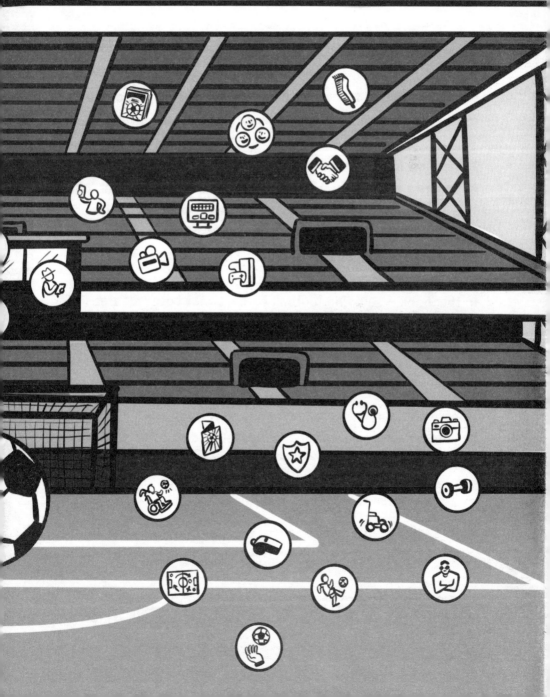

INTRODUCTION

Hi!

We're Dan and Daniel. We're good friends and we both LOVE football. And luckily, we both work in the industry too. When we're not writing this book, Daniel is busy being a sports and football lawyer and Dan is writing lots of football novels.

We feel so lucky to work in the game we love, and it inspired us to write this book for you, to show you all the brilliant jobs there are in the football industry. There are actually way more than 50 jobs in football, but we couldn't fit *them all* into one book so we've just included our top 50.

In this book, you'll find football careers that cover all areas of the game from action on the pitch to the business off it, a quiz to help you pick your path, and lots of fun clips to look up online (remember to ask an adult's permission before you do this).

However your mind works and no matter your skills, there will be someone like you working in football and so could you! Flick through the pages to discover how you can make football your future. Enjoy!

Dan Freedman and Daniel Geey

WITH SO MUCH AHEAD, WE CAN'T WAIT TO GET CRACKING.

WHILE THE EXCITEMENT IS HIGH, LET'S GET GOING.

WE'RE BUZZING FOR WHAT'S TO COME!

STADIUM ANNOUNCER

Lance Cook

Bristol Rovers FC

Announcing the goals to thousands of celebrating fans and playing the music at half-time – all from the best seat in the house – who wouldn't want to be a stadium announcer like Lance Cook?

 **01 STADIUM ANNOUNCER**

 LANCE COOK

- **Massive Bristol Rovers fan**

- **Is also a nightclub DJ!**

- **Reckons his job is the best in the world – maybe only second to being a player!**

INTERVIEW

What a brilliant job! How did you get started?

My dad knew the person who did the job before me at Bristol Rovers. We went to see him up in the box when I was about fifteen. I was massively into music, massively into football and I thought it was the coolest thing ever. First, I became the assistant, queuing the music, making sure the sound levels were right. Then, a few years later, I was lucky enough to get the job of being the announcer!

What's your schedule on match day like?

A lot of prep goes into it. It doesn't start just before the game. You spend a lot of time pulling together requests and information, writing the script and building the playlist – just making sure everything is in place.
Then, when we get to match day, it looks like this:

MATCH-DAY TIMELINE

1.30 P.M.
Arrive and kick things off with a playlist as the turnstiles open.

2.30 P.M.
Start my formal introductions, welcoming everyone to the game. Then we really build up the atmosphere to kick-off with loads of music and requests.

2.58 P.M.
The best bit – the teams coming out and me giving it big on the microphone!

3 P.M.
KICK-OFF

What do you say at half-time if the team is losing?

If we're losing, the atmosphere can be interesting. It's a massive responsibility because you can change the mood. You might get the music on a bit louder or you might say something to try to get the fans going, like: 'Let's give it for the boys! Forty-five minutes of non-stop noise!' That helps fans to remember that we're all in this together and we can do it. If you then hear that roar from the fans, it's brilliant.

Best and worst parts of the job?

The best has got to be that moment when the teams are coming out of the tunnel and you're welcoming everyone to the match. The crowd are going crazy, the walk-out tune's blaring and it's just like, *Yeah, this is why we do this.*

The worst part is obviously when you have a heavy defeat. The atmosphere isn't so great and you're helpless – those aren't fun afternoons.

Would you like to be an announcer for a different club?

Good question. Every time Rovers score a goal, I absolutely lose it on the mic. It's another really cool aspect of the job, being able to enjoy and elongate that goal. I don't know if I'd be able to do that if I was announcing for a club that I didn't support.

Could YOU do it?

The team you love is losing 2-0, and your job is to go down to the pitch at half-time and get the fans revved up and ready for the second half. Could you be inspirational and keep the crowd's mood high? If so, maybe you could be a stadium announcer!

GETTING THERE

Lance's top tips for following in his footsteps:

⚽ Write to your local club and show your interest. I'd always try to help if someone wrote to me.

⚽ When you go to a game, take notes. Figure out what's being said and when.

⚽ Be yourself.

⚽ Be clear and concise when reading aloud.

⚽ Be prepared for all eventualities. Mistakes happen. You're live out there in front of thousands of people, so you've just got to be prepared.

⚽ Ride the rollercoaster of emotions.

⚽ Studying English and drama will help with the key skills of speaking, listening, reading, writing and performing.

> 'GOOD LUCK! IF YOU CAN GET TO BE A STADIUM ANNOUNCER, IT'S AN ABSOLUTE PRIVILEGE. I WOULDN'T SWAP IT FOR THE WORLD!'

PHYSIOTHERAPIST

Caroline Woods

Northern Ireland Men's National Team

When a star player goes down injured, all eyes turn to one person – the physio.

CAROLINE WOODS

01 STADIUM ANNOUNCER

02 PHYSIOTHERAPIST

Comes from a horse-racing family – has been a jockey and a horse trainer

Can help both elite athletes and prize-winning horses

Studied to become a lawyer for five years before changing career

'I HAVE A LOVELY PHOTO, FROM OUR GAME AGAINST WALES, OF GARETH BALE WALKING BACK INTO THE CHANGING ROOM AND I'M WALKING BEHIND HIM WITH MY LITTLE MEDICAL BAG.'

INTERVIEW

What does a physiotherapist do?

My job is to support the players to be fully fit, physically and mentally, so they can perform to their very best on the pitch. We work closely with the doctor: they oversee things and we deliver the care.

What happens when there's an injury in the match?

I run on to the pitch. I'm mic'd up so I'm asking the other physio, who's got the game on the iPad, 'Can you see what happened? Can you give me a bit more detail?' That can tell us what sort of injury we're dealing with.

We'll also get information from the player and do our own assessment. Then we have to make the decision with coaching staff as to whether there needs to be a substitution. It can be an intense situation.

There might be a rowdy crowd or opposition players putting you under pressure. That's why I don't like it when my friends text me to say that they saw me on television – it means someone got injured.

What was your big break?

I got a master's degree in sports medicine in Dublin and I knew I wanted to work in football but I didn't have any football connections. So I wrote to 92 clubs and I got four replies. Two said, thanks, but no thanks; one explained that they had nothing at the moment but would keep my details on file . . . and the fourth one was Bristol City. They said they needed a physio to work in the academy and asked me to go over and visit. I thought, *Brilliant, I will!*

I packed up my little car and off I went to Bristol. That was it. Once you get your foot in the door, you're good to go.

What's been the highlight of your career so far?

Every time I meet up with the national team is a real privilege – but the highlight was definitely Euro 2016. Northern Ireland hadn't qualified for a major tournament in 30 years, so it felt like it could be a once-in-a-lifetime experience. It was in France and we had the most fantastic base camp, and then just so many great moments. Rory McIlroy came into the changing room, which was special. We qualified for the knockout stage, the Eiffel Tower was lit up with a big football on it . . . The whole thing was just amazing and I was lucky enough to be sitting pitchside to watch it all.

GETTING THERE

If you'd like to follow in Caroline's footsteps, here's her checklist of what you'll need:

⚽ Be good under pressure. We're dealing with players who are very valuable and, as well as being vital to the national team, also have their responsibilities to their clubs, so decision-making in those circumstances is key.

⚽ Be ready for long hours. When I meet up with the team, it's 24/7 for the entire duration.

⚽ Be a really good communicator. You'll need to explain your diagnosis, recovery timescales and treatment plans to the players, coaches and their clubs. Always keep those lines of communication open.

⚽ Be flexible. If you're working with a smaller team or club, you might not have lots of staff, facilities or equipment, so you need to prioritise and be prepared to put your own needs aside to support the players and the team.

⚽ Be committed and reliable. People are counting on you. In the medical department, there's no room for excuses as to why you weren't there.

⚽ Be prepared to volunteer. If I saw that someone had been sacrificing their spare time from a young age to do work experience and learn from other physios, they would be the kind of person I'd want on my team.

⚽ Enjoy it. You're involved in sport – and it's your job! You're getting paid to do what other people would do for free. It's pretty special.

BARBER

Smokey

Smokey has cut the hair of some of the best players in the world. But his story goes far deeper . . .

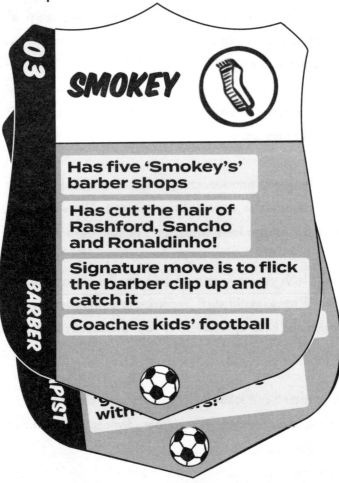

03

BARBER

...PIST

SMOKEY

Has five 'Smokey's' barber shops

Has cut the hair of Rashford, Sancho and Ronaldinho!

Signature move is to flick the barber clip up and catch it

Coaches kids' football

...with ...rs!

'NO STRUGGLE, NO PROGRESS. KEEP WORKING HARD AND DON'T TAKE NO FOR AN ANSWER. YOU NEVER KNOW WHEN IT COULD BE YOU.'

INTERVIEW

Where did you learn to be a barber?

I taught myself in jail, cutting inmates' hair and trying to get better. For me, it wasn't about being a good barber inside there, it was more about the inmates coming to me to talk about their problems. I was good at listening and trying to give them advice. Later on, I tried to master my craft, and I got good at it and enjoyed it. Now it's my career.

What's it like cutting the hair of all those top players?

I don't look at them as footballers. These are human beings. They're going to be happy, sad and going through problems, just like anyone else. You can't start treating them in a different way. If something's not right, I'll let them know that. But if something's good, I'll let them know that too. It's all about human relationships.

Does everything you've been through in your life give you that courage to tell people the truth?

Sometimes people hide their past. I don't do that. My past is the reason I am who I am. When people ask me about my life, straight away I say, 'Yep, I've been to jail – this is where I started.' I was in the wrong place at the wrong time, but at the same time you have to take accountability for your actions.

Telling the truth takes you a long way. If you don't like me, you don't like me. You don't have to use my services. But if I'm being truthful and you respect what I'm saying then our relationship will be superb. My experience has taught me a lot in terms of seeing people for who they are. I always say I'm on this planet for a reason, so if I see a young kid going down the wrong path and I can guide them because I've been through it, then I'm going to do it.

IF IT WERE YOU?

IF YOU BECAME A FAMOUS BARBER WHAT WOULD BE YOUR SIGNATURE MOVE AND TRADEMARK LOOK?

It sounds like you play an important role in your clients' lives.

A lot of people have got a lot going on and they see their barber as a counsellor, someone they can talk to who's not going to judge them or tell anyone else their secrets or problems. You have to give people space and time, where they can rant and let go of what's holding them back. Sometimes people need to let it out and what you need to do is just listen. That helps a lot of people.

What's been the craziest moment?

Getting the chance to meet my idol, Ronaldinho, and cutting his hair. We were in a room for two hours, just me and him, talking. He spoke only a little English, and I don't speak Portuguese, but it was about adapting to the scenario. Somehow, for two hours, we were conversing. It didn't matter what we were talking about. We made it make sense.

Your shops have a special vibe. Apart from cutting people's hair, what is it you're trying to achieve?

We're in an era where people can't even talk to each other on trains. At Smokey's Barbers we want teenagers coming in and talking. I normally have seven seats in each shop, purposely because I want people to have to talk. You've got seven different people from different places, different cultures, different ages, but we could share the same conversation. It could be football, but it could be about life at home. OK, let's hear what the kid's got to say, let's hear what the parent's got to say. Everyone's got an opinion and when you have those opinions up in the air, it educates the young generation, so it's good for them to hear and be involved in these conversations in the barber's.

GETTING THERE

Here are Smokey's top tips for being a great barber:

⚽ Do your best to make your clients happy – go above and beyond for them.

⚽ Make sure you understand what haircut they want before you start – hair is important.

⚽ As well as being good at cutting hair, you've got to be a good listener.

⚽ The focus is all on the client and how you're making them feel. Ask them questions.

PRESENTER
Reshmin Chowdhury

What's it like being on TV, presenting the biggest football matches in the world?

03

04

PRESENTER

RESHMIN CHOWDHURY

Used to sing in her spare time

Did the first interview with Ronaldo when he joined Real Madrid

Presented the FIFA World Cup draw, alongside Idris Elba

'WHETHER YOU'RE PRESENTING TO ONE PERSON OR A MILLION PEOPLE, IT'S THE SAME THING. JUST BE YOUR BEST SELF.'

INTERVIEW

Did you always want to be a football presenter?

I grew up in a Bengali family where education was the priority. But my passion for football was everything to me.

However, if you told me at the age of eleven that I would be presenting a World Cup, I'd just think it was impossible. When I started, the pathway to being a football presenter was closed unless you knew someone. For me – being Asian and being a woman – there was just no way. I was on the outside and it wasn't a world that I ever felt I could be a part of.

How did you make it happen?

I studied politics and started producing the news, hoping to be a news presenter. I learned Spanish too, so I had that up my sleeve.

And then I saw an advert for Real Madrid TV. I wasn't sure about living in Spain but I thought I'd just go for it and see what happened.

I ended up getting the job and then it all went from there. Although it sounds simple, it was the building blocks that I'd put in place that allowed me to take the opportunity when it came:

- **I had a qualification in journalism**
- **I had studied languages**
- **I had experience in being a producer and had put myself out there**

These things meant that when my chance arrived, I was ready.

What's been your best moment so far?

I was able to host a chat between Messi and Ronaldo at the UEFA Champions League draw. We had planned to speak to each player separately, but I knew both of them and I wanted to do something for the fans.

We went off-script: Ronaldo had just moved to Italy and I asked, 'Do you miss each other?' The rest of it came through their conversation – it was a really iconic moment, one of the last times we saw them together at their peak.

What would you say to someone who feels like they won't be given a chance because of their race or religion?

Don't ever let your identity hold you back – and don't lose your identity. That's such a huge mistake! Celebrate it. You are who you are because you're uniquely you. If you're a little bit different, you have a unique perspective and you can bring that into every conversation. If you're from a family with dual heritage, for example, you really have a different way of relating to people.

GETTING THERE

Reshmin's advice on how to become a presenter:

 The energy you transmit to the audience is very important – sometimes as important as the content.

⚽ Think about what the audience want from the programme and ask the questions they want to know the answers to. If a manager is under pressure, the focus should be on what the root of the problem is. Where does the club go from here?

⚽ You never know what's going to be useful down the line, so learn as many skills as you can. Languages will open doors for you: I've spoken to Zidane in French and Messi in Spanish. Speaking in their language allows you to naturally relate to players.

⚽ Many people will make you feel that you can't do it. So you've got to have that inner steel and confidence to go for it.

⚽ Find your passion. Find your value. Find your tribe. And find the people who bring out the best in you.

⚽ Stay humble and be nice. Not because of what you want from people, but because it's the right thing to do. You've got to be a team player.

⚽ Go into it because you're passionate, not because you want to be famous or rich. Be yourself and, if you're good at what you do, things will happen.

● ● ○ FIND IT ONLINE! ✖

Search: 'Messi & Ronaldo's interview at UCL draw' - you'll see Reshmin speaking to the GOATs (in Spanish and English!).

LET'S GO

ARCHITECT
Rita Ochoa

Imagine going to a massive football match, sitting in a brand-new stadium and seeing thousands of people enjoying the event around you. Now imagine being the person who designed the stadium! Rita Ochoa is an architect who specialises in exactly that . . .

05

ARCHITECT

RITA OCHOA

From Lisbon, Portugal

Worked on Brentford FC's stadium and the extension to Barcelona's Camp Nou stadium

INTERVIEW

Did you always want to be a football architect?

Actually, I come from a family that has no interest in football. Every time there was a match on TV, we'd change to another channel. I wanted to be a film-maker; that was my dream. But I'd always liked architecture too and I realised it's not that different from film-making, because in both cases what you're doing is creating the set for the story to unfold.

What was your big break?

When Portugal hosted Euro 2004, the country needed to build lots of new stadiums from scratch. I happened to be a student at one of the architecture firms involved in building lots of them, so it gave me a chance to learn.

What's special about your job?

Football stadiums are like churches or temples or festivals: they are for everyone. When you go to a match, you can sit next to someone who's very wealthy or a child or an old person. People from all these different backgrounds and – with the emotion of the game – they can all end up singing together. It's almost religious. Where else do you find this in the world? I really enjoy what I do.

Which stadium are you most proud of?

Brentford's stadium is my most recent baby. It was a unique experience trying to design something new, which would be accepted by the fans, and that would also fit into a triangular site surrounded by three railways. We also had to build half of the construction during Covid and we had very specific requirements from the client, so I am very proud of this building and the team that worked on it.

'AN ARCHITECT IS ALWAYS IMAGINING NOT JUST THE BUILDINGS, BUT ALSO THE STORIES THAT CAN HAPPEN WITHIN THEM.'

How does it feel going to a match in a stadium you've designed?

I usually go to the first match or event, and I always cry. It's so emotional because you know every detail and the years that it has taken to build the stadium. You imagine the players going into the dressing room you have designed. You see the building in a level of detail that no one else could imagine.

DID YOU KNOW?

Artificial intelligence and virtual reality are both key elements of modern architecture, as well as drawing by hand, which comes at the beginning of the process.

Have YOU got the SKILLS?

To be a football architect, you'll need to be good at:

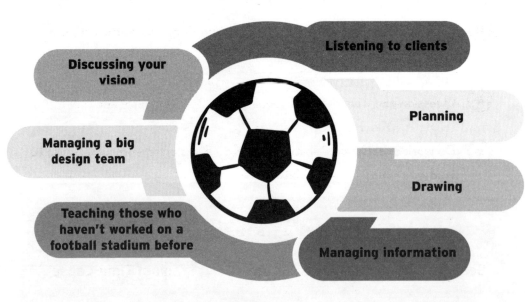

Listening to clients

Discussing your vision

Planning

Managing a big design team

Drawing

Teaching those who haven't worked on a football stadium before

Managing information

GETTING THERE

Here are Rita's top tips for becoming an architect:

- Draw whenever you can. Always have a notepad with you and draw whatever you see or imagine. Don't worry if the drawings aren't good – no one will see them, but the more you practise, the more you'll develop. I've met so many kids who learned to draw by watching YouTube videos.

- Get good grades. Architecture is a difficult course to get into, so you'll need good marks.

- Understand the world. It's not just about being good at maths or drawing: the more knowledge you have, the better you'll be. If you know about music, you'll understand arenas. If you know about history, maybe one day you'll work on a restoration.

- Travel and visit different buildings around the world. Go to galleries – they will give you inspiration.

- Look up. When you walk through any building, look at the ceiling and assess the proportions. Why is this different from my house?

- Question the world around you. Why are things built – and how?

- Do work experience. Most architecture firms offer work experience to students over the age of sixteen.

● ● ● FIND IT ONLINE! ✕

Search: 'Two Years in Two Minutes! New Stadium Time-Lapse'.

HEAD COACH

Will Still

Stade de Reims

You don't need to have been a world-class player to become a world-class coach. Will Still believes his unique pathway has helped him to become the coach he is today.

05 06

WILL STILL

Born in Belgium but has English parents

Speaks English, Dutch and French

Became the manager of the French team Stade de Reims at only thirty years old!

'I THOUGHT: IF I CAN'T BE A PLAYER, I'LL PUT CONES OUT, WASH THE BOOTS . . . I'LL EVEN CLEAN THE KIT IF I HAVE TO – AS LONG AS I CAN WORK IN FOOTBALL.'

INTERVIEW

How do you see your role as a head coach?

I try to get the best out of football players, for them to win as many games as possible, so that I can stay in a job for as long as possible. To achieve this, I put on training sessions to help each player improve, and therefore the team becomes better.

I'm judged on results. If you lose, you're struggling and you're in trouble, and if you win, you're the best person in the world and an absolute genius. That's the life of a head coach.

Did you always want to be a coach?

I wanted to be a footballer and played at semi-professional level. Around the age of twenty, I realised I wasn't going to make it. I was desperate to work in football and approached a young, dynamic Belgian coach called Yannick Ferrera. To this day, I have no idea how I found the courage to walk up and talk to him. That conversation changed my life because he gave me a job as a video analyst and allowed me to take my first steps in professional football. Watching him, I was like, 'Yeah, that's what I want to do.'

Can you tell us about your life growing up?

Being a little kid growing up in Belgium, it was easy to take the mickey out of me because I spoke English and stood out because of my bright orange hair. But I was the best at football, so people wanted to talk to me and be part of my team. It's been part of my life ever since.

Have those experiences made you a better coach?

Being seen as different when you're a kid opens your eyes. For example, if I'm working with a player who has come to the club from abroad and is discovering a new league, environment and language, I know what it feels like and I know how long it can take to adapt.

I also know how coaches treated me when they put me on the bench or took me out of the squad. Sometimes they didn't explain it or say anything to me. It was really hard but I learned so much from it. Now, as a coach myself, I'd never want to do that to one of my players.

HARDEST PART

Sometimes you have to miss out on things, like parties, because of work. Plus, some people will think you're not doing a good enough job and that's hard to hear.

GETTING THERE

Will's top tips for becoming a coach:

⚽ Watch and listen to what the experts say about the games. What are the teams doing well?

⚽ Start practising your own coaching as soon as you can. Organise sessions and think about how you're going to make other people better.

⚽ Be determined. Don't let people tell you that you're not good enough or that it's never going to work. You will have failures, but make sure you learn from them and move on.

⚽ Go with your instincts. If you think a player is worth the time and energy to develop, then do it.

⚽ See the game from as many angles as possible. When you're playing, ask lots of questions and try to understand why your coach is making certain decisions. Or even try refereeing to understand the game from that perspective too.

● ● ● FIND IT ONLINE! ✕

Search: 'Will Still: The Football Manager Genius Who's Managed vs Mbappé and Messi' to see Will talk about his football journey.

LET'S GO

CLUB OWNER

Ben Robinson MBE

Burton Albion FC

Imagine actually owning your own football club. It's only possible if you're a multibillionaire and come from a different country, right? Wrong. Ben Robinson was a local boy who ended up owning Burton Albion FC.

07

CLUB OWNER

BEN ROBINSON MBE

- Was scouted by Burton Albion
- Was a successful businessman before buying the club
- His grandson wants him to sign Messi for Burton Albion!

INTERVIEW

How did you become the owner of Burton Albion?

I grew up in Burton-on-Trent during the Second World War. My mother, Edna-May was a white working-class local girl and she fell in love with my father, a Black American GI (soldier), whose name was Clarence Pettiford. After the war, he went back to the States and I was brought up by my mum and my stepfather.

I met two of the directors of Burton Albion through my career in business. They asked me to help the club by increasing its sponsorship and advertising revenues – so that's how I got involved, and eventually I bought the club.

As owner of the club, everything is your responsibility. How often do you speak to your manager, for example?

I don't have day-to-day conversations with my manager and I never have. I believe an owner should stick to the side of the club where their skill set applies. OK, there are times when you have a run of bad results, and you ask the manager to explain what the problem is and how they are going to turn it round. Generally, though, as an owner, you give the manager a job, and then you support them.

To own a football club, you need to be good at business. Do you have any business tips for us?

Throughout my life, whenever I meet people, I've never been interested in how many Rolls-Royces they own, or anything materialistic – I've been interested in their mindset and their strategy. You can learn so much just by talking to others. It's not you telling them what you've done, but instead using the opportunity to learn from them.

What does a day in the life of a football club owner look like?

My role is chairman, owner, chief executive, general dogsbody – whatever needs to be done – so my days are very practical.

- **I have meetings with all the different departments in the club. They all come to me to have a chat. The sponsorship department may ask if we can do a special deal for a regular customer**

- **Then our accounts department will update me on our finances,**

- **I might have a chat with the manager about accommodation for upcoming games. There are costs involved, which you have to weigh up . . .**

- **Finally, at the end of the day, you can often find me going around switching all the lights off in the building!**

What's the best part about owning a football club?

We reached the semi-final of the EFL Cup against Man City and we've had amazing experiences in the FA Cup too, but for me the biggest satisfaction comes from the community element of the club and the power of sport. We're not Manchester United. We're a little club and we run it for the community. I've given the NHS the use of the stadium as a vaccination centre and they have now delivered 750,000 vaccinations for Covid and the flu.

Every Sunday morning, I come into the office and the car park is rammed with hundreds and hundreds of cars. You look at the 3G pitch and there's all age groups. And it's not just the fact that the kids are playing football; they are also developing their personalities and their outlook on life. I think that's so important.

GETTING THERE

If your ambition is to follow in Ben's footsteps and be a football club owner, he has some great advice:

- ⚽ **If you really want to be successful, you've got to always be prepared to work. If you're lazy, it's going to be twice as hard to achieve your goals.**

- ⚽ **It's also about attitude. Think about what you want to achieve and how you can best make it happen. That starts with how you spend each day of your life.**

- ⚽ **Never be afraid to ask questions and seek good advice.**

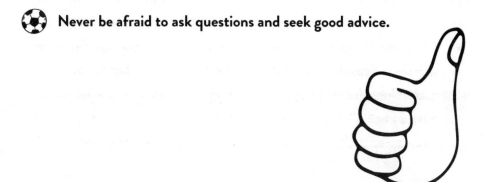

GROUNDSKEEPER
Tara Sandford

The football pitch is where the players work – but who looks after the pitches?

> 'SOMETIMES I WALKED ABOUT THINKING IT COULDN'T BE REAL, THIS COULDN'T BE MY LIFE.'

08

GROUNDSKEEPER

TARA SANDFORD

She was the first female groundsperson to work for Arsenal

Worked at both the Arsenal training ground and the Emirates Stadium

A massive Arsenal fan!

INTERVIEW

Can you tell us what you did for Arsenal?

My main role was to maintain the pitches at the Arsenal Training Ground. The groundstaff cut the grass – making sure it's the height that the manager wants – and get the strips in the pitch looking nice and neat. They paint the lines, spray the pesticides and clear the leaves. They also look after the gardens, so they do planting, make the borders and cut the hedges.

Sounds great! So, you were around the players every day?

Yes, I used to see them day in, day out. It was my job to make everything look good for them and they appreciated it. They were lovely, and everyone said hello. It's one big group and I loved just being around the club. Knowing I was part of the team I've supported all my life was special. I'm very appreciative and very lucky that I got to work there.

Did you get to watch training?

Sometimes we had to take equipment off the pitches at the end of training, so we often had five or ten minutes watching the players before they finished. They're all world class and it was a joy to watch them.

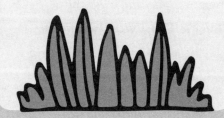

How did you get such a unique job?

I'm not an office person. I like being outside, doing something practical. When I was little, I'd always be helping my dad in the garden. I loved being in the sunshine with my family, making things look nice. It was something we bonded over. But I didn't know then that gardening was a job; I just thought it was something you did at the weekend.

After searching for what I wanted to do, I managed to get a job at the council, looking after the public green spaces. I did it for about seven years and got an apprenticeship in horticulture (growing plants for food and medicine). I loved it. Then I saw an advertisement for a job at Arsenal. Going to the interview, I was probably the most nervous I've ever been in my life. But I got the callback the same day, offering me the job.

ACCIDENTAL STAR

'The in-house media team do a Carpool Karaoke with the players at the training ground. Alessia Russo was doing one and I accidentally got in the background of it!'

You're one of very few female groundskpeepers. If there's a girl reading this who wants to do what you do, what would you say to her?

If it's something that interests you, just go for it. Don't worry what other people think. Go to college, learn the trade, listen to your gut and believe in yourself. I was part of the first all-women grounds team to prepare a Women's Super League match, which was hugely exciting for me on both a personal and professional level. The consistent level of support Arsenal have seen for the women's team shows how much the game continues to grow, and it's important that we harness this to encourage more girls to pursue a career in football at all levels.

GETTING THERE

These are Tara's top tips if you'd like to follow in her footsteps:

- ⚽ Have great attention to detail. You're working for a top club, so everything needs to look pristine.

- ⚽ Be prepared for long hours. In the summer we might not finish until 10 p.m.

- ⚽ Be professional. Sometimes inside I might be like, 'Oh my God, Bukayo Saka's just walked past me,' but you can't show it. This is your job.

- ⚽ Be ready to learn. I'm studying irrigation and draining at the moment. I enjoy that process of taking on new information.

- ⚽ Be confident. I wasn't sure if I was good enough to do this job or if I had the right experience, but it's worked out well for me – and it can for you, too.

● ● ○ FIND IT ONLINE! ✕

Search: 'Carpool Alessia Russo & Frimmy' and you'll see Tara pop up in the background at 4 minutes 38 seconds!

LET'S GO

EVENT MANAGER

Tom Fehler

UEFA

Have you ever tried organising a club football match? There can be quite a few things to think about. Now imagine it's your job to organise the biggest football match on the planet: the UEFA Champions League final.

09

EVENT MANAGER

TOM FEHLER

Tom and his team manage the Champions League final event

It's watched by 450 million people around the world!

He started out as a football coach

INTERVIEW

So, all your work revolves around the Champions League final?

That's right. Sometimes people think, *It's just a football match, why do you need a year to plan it?* But there are so many different elements that need to be organised: the fans, the clubs, the players, the media, the stadium, the host city, the ticketing, the entertainment, the safety . . . All these different areas make up the final. There are a lot of plans to go through. The level of detail that goes into it is huge – it's the best around.

CHAMPIONS LEAGUE TIMELINE

Planning starts around 18 months before the match kicks off.

Bids are assessed by UEFA.

When the tournament reaches the quarter-final stage, Tom and his team meet with all the clubs to discuss the plans for the final.

All the national football associations bid to host the final.

The UEFA Executive Committee makes the decision on where the final will be.

Sounds like an incredible job! How close to the football do you get?

You certainly have a lot of contact with the clubs and then you're pitchside around the players during the build-up and the post-match trophy ceremony. I'm very privileged to do it, and in my career I have met and worked with people like David Beckham, Gareth Southgate and Harry Kane – but it's also important to remember that you're there to work and not get too distracted by it. Seeing the winning captain lift the Champions League trophy just in front of you is one of the most enjoyable moments. You do all the hard work in the planning and preparation, and then you see it all come together – those are the moments you really enjoy.

Are there any downsides?

You have to be prepared for the negatives; for example, if something goes wrong, it will get more news headlines than if it all went right. Sometimes that can be difficult.

Also, if you're focusing on turnstile operations, or waste management, or fencing arrangements, you might not feel you're directly involved in the football, but these elements are vital to the event too. Despite this, I love my job and would recommend it to anyone wanting to work close to football.

Could YOU do it?

To be an event organiser, you'll need to be:

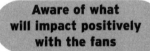

Good with people

Aware of what will impact positively with the fans

Able to adapt your personality to different situations

Hard-working and with good attention to detail

Committed and prepared to give a lot of your own time

Constantly thinking of the bigger picture and planning for the worst

Calm in high-pressure situations

GETTING THERE

Here's Tom advice if you'd like to one day be the person organising a Champions League final:

⚽ Even if you know the exact thing you want to do, have a go at doing something else first. Volunteering and coaching really helped to build my experience. It's not always the case that you can have everything all at once. You may need to take a few sidesteps to progress, and the other jobs you do will give you some key skills.

⚽ It involves a lot of persistence and a lot of hard work – never be put off and think anything is too big. When I was volunteering, I was always aspiring to work on something like the Champions League final in the future. Opportunities will come up if push yourself and have a focus on where you want to be. You can really do anything you want to.

NEXT STEPS?

Have a go at organising your own football tournament or party. You'll need to consider many of the same elements in the planning as you would if you were organising a big football match, so you'll be learning the foundations.

STADIUM TOUR GUIDE

Alex O'Donnell

Celtic FC

ALEX O'DONNELL

STADIUM TOUR GUIDE

First got involved with Celtic through the Ability Counts programme when he was eleven

Used to be a club mascot

Now also a coach

Going to your club's home ground is a special moment for any fan but some people get to do that every day as their job!

'ALEX IS ABSOLUTELY PHENOMENAL FOR US. HE IS A REAL EXAMPLE OF WHAT CAN BE ACHIEVED IF YOU LIVE WITH A DISABILITY.'

TONY HAMILTON – CHIEF EXECUTIVE, CELTIC FC FOUNDATION

INTERVIEW

What's a typical day as a stadium tour guide like?

I get up at 8.15 a.m. I wear my Celtic blazer and tie, and I put my lanyard on – I always look very smart. Mum drives me to the club and I check in at reception.

I know my way around the whole stadium and I've got my pass that lets me go everywhere I need to go.

The tour starts at 11 a.m. I meet the guests and start taking them around. The first place we go is the trophy room. We have time for photos because everyone likes their photo with the European Cup.

Then we go into the changing rooms. Everyone is always very excited: it's the most special, secret place in the football club. I always feel excited too.

Then we go out on to the pitch. I like that part: I show them all the seats, and the people get to sit in the dugout and take more photos. The tour lasts for 60 minutes and there are usually about 40 people on it.

Your Celtic suit sounds cool! How much did it cost?

They gave me the blazer with the badge on it for free, which was very nice. Celtic is like my family. They all look after me.

FUNNY MOMENT

I once bumped into Ange Postecoglou and I said, 'Oh, it's Big Ange!' And he said, 'Thanks, mate.' I had a big cheesy smile on my face. He's a very kind man.

Lots of people know you at the club and you've been interviewed by Sky Sports and FIFA too. Are you famous?

Ha ha! I suppose I'm a bit of a star. Mainly I'm just a huge fan. I memorise all the team players and numbers. People on the tour can say a number and I can tell them what player wears that shirt. Or if they tell me the player's name, I can tell them his shirt number. Callum McGregor is number 42. James Forrest is number 49 – that's a very easy one. I can probably go back as far as maybe five or ten years ago.

Who's your favourite player?

Callum McGregor is one of my favourites and I also like Fraser Forster. I met him at an Ability Counts football programme. He's very tall – I'm about 1.7 metres and I think he's about 2 metres! We went on a tour of Lennoxtown; we did some training.

For my twenty-first birthday party some of the Celtic players made a video for me, wishing me a happy birthday. Callum McGregor was in the video, and so were James Forrest and Odsonne Édouard. It was very good. And they also gave me a signed T-shirt.

What's been your happiest moment in football?

I'm always happy when I'm playing. I'm a goalkeeper and I've won a couple of trophies. Sometimes I get picked as Player of the Match – that's wonderful.

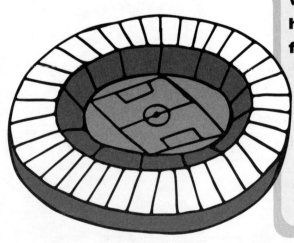

Have YOU got the SKILLS?

To be a stadium tour guide, you'll need to be:

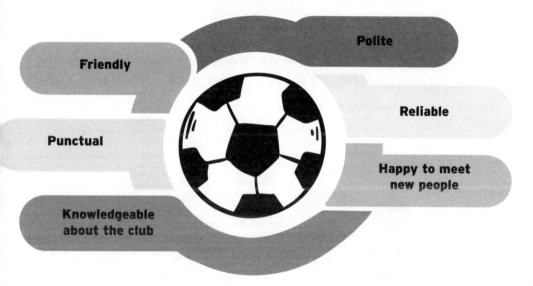

- Polite
- Friendly
- Reliable
- Punctual
- Happy to meet new people
- Knowledgeable about the club

We asked Alex and his dad, Owen, what advice they'd give to someone who would like to follow in Alex's footsteps . . .

ALEX: Follow your passion and believe in yourself.

OWEN: Anything is possible – don't restrict yourself. It's about ability, not disability.

FIND IT ONLINE! ✖

Search: 'Celtic fan inspires on World Down Syndrome Day' to see Sky Sports' video of Alex doing what he loves at Celtic.

LET'S GO

HEAD OF COMMUNITY

Clare Martin MBE

Portsmouth FC

Football clubs play a massive role in the local community, supporting millions of people at all stages of their lives. Wearing the club badge and helping those around you is a hugely rewarding job.

11

HEAD OF COMMUNITY

CLARE MARTIN MBE

One of the best-known faces in Portsmouth

Helping to develop a new sports facility in Portsmouth

Has an MBE for her work for Pompey in the Community

INTERVIEW

What does your job entail?

I head up the charity that works with Portsmouth Football Club. We run sports, education, health, inclusion and disability projects in Portsmouth and the surrounding areas. Our aim is to find a way for anybody, of any age, and whatever their ability, to do something positive connected to Portsmouth Football Club.

For example, each week during term time we deliver coaching and training programmes to over 6,000 students and pupils. It's a very busy job. Every day is completely different, and I think that's why so many people who work in the charity here love it.

Do the results on the pitch affect the community?

Massively. It's tangible across the city when we're doing well. We've got 180,000 people in the city, and when we won the FA Cup in 2008, we had 250,000 on the common. Even people who say they're not Pompey fans – they might be fans of a big Premier League club –are all Pompey underneath. They've all got blue blood.

As you work with so many people in the community, does everyone in Portsmouth know you?

Yes, my kids hate it! When we did the Great South Run, which is a 10 mile run through Portsmouth, literally every 50 yards I was saying hello to somebody because my role is so high profile within our area. The football club is where people want to be.

It's amazing, considering the fact that I wasn't even a football fan when I grew up. Girls weren't allowed to play when I was at school. I don't think I ever kicked a ball until I started working here. I was teaching at a local school and we were given some tickets through the club, so I took a minibus full of children down. I had to ask what colour we were playing in, because

I didn't even know that. But I loved it, and I was hooked from that day. In terms of working with the club, I was originally recruited as a teacher to run the study centre. I've been here 23 years now. It's a privilege – I feel very honoured.

IS IT FOR YOU?

Every day is different when you work for a club community organisation. Would you like to do these activities?

MONDAY	Working with pupils in a primary school on the Premier League Primary Stars programme
TUESDAY	Working with the first team on a healthy-eating project
WEDNESDAY	Working with people studying for a football coaching degree
THURSDAY	Taking players to the local hospital to visit people who aren't well
FRIDAY	Organising a girls' football competition, followed by an after-school junior disability football session
SATURDAY	Organising the mascots and flag-wavers for match day

Tell us about one of your most memorable moments in the job . . .

To recognise the work we do here, I got an MBE, which was incredible. And then, because of that, I was also invited to the Queen's funeral – being front row in front of five billion people watching around the world . . . That was something I'll never forget.

What are the downsides?

It's hard work. We don't get much funding, so everything we do, we have to earn or we have to bid for. I've got 56 people working in the charity and it's up to me to find the money to pay their salaries every month.

GETTING THERE

Here are Clare's tips:

 Our website and social media pages are full of ideas, activities and programmes that we're running. Come along, take part in some activities and then start volunteering. It's not just about being there, it's about getting involved.

●●○ FIND IT ONLINE!

Search: 'Portsmouth teach local kids how to cook' to see Clare and her team coaching local kids on how to pick up some top cooking skills!

LET'S GO

TIPS FROM THE TOP

'I'm living proof of the different ways you can be part of football. I thought I'd be a professional but ended up becoming an agent and now I work with incredible players. I'm achieving my football dream in another way.' **TOBI ALABI - football agent**

'Find something you want to achieve and then be relentless towards that goal. Stay consistent at something every day for one to two years and you will 100% get there.' **JEMAL WISEMAN - former pro footballer, now junior software engineer at Football Manager**

'Work hard, do everything with a smile and let your love of the game take you as far as you can go.'
ELLA TOONE - England Lioness

'If you're going for an interview , here are a few tips:

1. Be on time - if you're not early, you're late!
2. Try to smile and relax
3. Look smart - first impressions count!
4. Don't be frightened to ask a question at the end

Football is an exciting industry to work in. Good luck!' **DAVID DEIN MBE - one of the founding fathers of the Premier League**

'Love of the sport is great but the industry needs skills off the pitch as well as on it, so exam results and work experience matter. We need new people from all backgrounds, so don't worry if you think you won't "fit in".'
PHIL SMITH - Sport England

ADVICE FROM YOUR BIGGEST SUPPORTERS IN THE GAME

'Drop any fear of failure and give it your all. If you don't, you will never know if it could have worked out. So dream big – and know that this is an industry for everyone!' **LEON MANN MBE – managing director and founder of the Black Collective of Media in Sport and co-founder of the Football Black List**

'Working in football is also a celebration of the past and how the game has brought people together. Don't forget how much football can change lives.' **JANE BATEMAN – head of international relations at the FA and deputy chair of trustees at the National Football Museum**

'Never be afraid to tell – and show – people how much you want an opportunity. Be prepared to demonstrate your hunger, passion and desire to stand out from the crowd.' **ALAN SHEARER CBE – all-time Premier League leading goalscorer**

'Working together with everybody is key in any football job. Remember, you're part of a big community that loves the game as much as you do. Be patient, keep practising, and you might just make it.' **SHARON BRITTAN – club chairman, Bolton Wanderers**

'Education is your only insurance. Pursue your football but don't forget your education because you might need it one day. I say the same thing to you that I always say to Reece and Lauren: Do your very best and be proud of yourself.' **NIGEL JAMES – Elite coach and dad of Reece and Lauren James**

'My mantra is: Leave things better than you found them. Remember, you are in control of your future and you get to choose how you learn and grow.' **RUTH SHAW OBE – chief executive, Premier League Charitable Fund**

'You need to be determined because it takes a lot to make it in the football business. Football is a people business so you need to be able to connect.' **NEERAV PAREKH – owner of Barnsley FC**

'Work hard. Those who reach the top aren't necessarily the most talented – but they are the hardest working. They're also the most trustworthy. Trust means everything.' **HENRY WINTER – Football Journalist of the Year**

'I have often said that football saved my life, providing me with a safe space where I could be free and dream. Believe in yourself, work hard and anything is possible.' **PAUL MCNEILL – head of football development, Scottish FA**

'What I love most about football is how it teaches you about life. The ability to face setbacks, communicate with others and embrace different cultures are skills that will help you achieve great things – on and off the pitch.' **KIT BROWN – teacher, semi-pro footballer, author and TikTok star**

KICK-OFF

IT'S TIME FOR KICK-OFF AND SO WE'RE GOING TO BE LOOKING AT THE JOBS ON THE FIELD, IN THE STADIUM AND BEHIND THE SCENES.

YOU MAY THINK A GAME OF FOOTBALL IS ALL ABOUT THE MATCH ITSELF, BUT TO MAKE THE MATCH HAPPEN, THERE ARE HUNDREDS OF PEOPLE WORKING HARD TO KEEP THE TEAM FIT, KEEP THE LIGHTS ON AND LOOK AFTER THE FANS.

GET READY TO MEET THE TEAM BEHIND THE TEAM.

COMMENTATOR
Seb Hutchinson

Imagine being the voice of the game: your words being the soundtrack to huge matches, great goals and incredible pieces of action. What a job! Seb Hutchinson is a football commentator on radio and TV, having dreamt of doing the job since the age of ten.

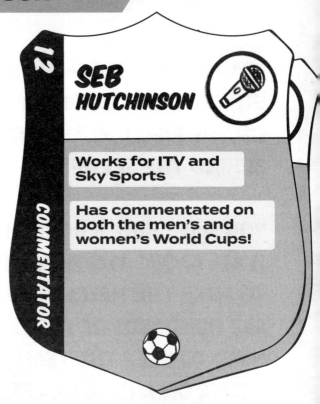

12

COMMENTATOR

SEB HUTCHINSON

Works for ITV and Sky Sports

Has commentated on both the men's and women's World Cups!

INTERVIEW

Why did you want to be a commentator?

As a kid, I'd watch tournaments on TV and being a commentator seemed like a great job. I got that ambition when I was eleven or twelve, and never wavered from

it. That's a big part of it – if you know what you want to do early on, you're halfway there.

What was your big break?

I did a course in sports broadcast

journalism. Then I sent a showreel (a video showcasing my work) to loads of companies. ITV responded and I started there as a junior producer. It was a brilliant start in TV.

Best part of the job?

You get to watch something you love and be at the big events, including the World Cup! Lots of people are watching and you get to be the narrator. It's a lovely role.

Hardest parts?

There are a lot of matches on weekends and evenings, so you're always working when people are off. Also, anyone working in the public eye can receive criticism, and that can be very hard.

BEST MOMENT

Patrick Schick's long-range goal for the Czech Republic against Scotland at the Euros in 2022. He was on the halfway line so you wouldn't necessarily have thought he was going to shoot, but I recognised it was on for him and went big on it – and I was glad I did, because he executed a top-class piece of skill on the big stage.

THEY THINK IT'S ALL OVER

Possibly the most famous bit of commentary was said by Kenneth Wolstenholme in the last few seconds of the match in which England won the World Cup in 1966:

'Some people on the pitch! They think it's all over . . .' he said.

'IT IS NOW!'

MATCH-DAY TIMELINE

STEP 1 — Arrive at the ground three hours before kick-off.

STEP 2 — Pick up media pass. Go to check out the commentary position.

STEP 3 — If it's a TV game, chat to producers, director, presenter and pundits (former players) to get that feeling of being part of a team.

STEP 4 — Back to the commentary position 90 minutes before kick-off to get the team news.

STEP 5 — Make notes on the headlines from the team news and work out the formations.

STEP 6 — Watch the warm-ups to see how everything's shaping up.

STEP 7 — GAME TIME!

IS IT FOR YOU?

Can you imagine sitting in the commentary box, with producers and directors talking to you through your headphones . . . a pundit sat next to you, having their say . . . the pressure of millions of people watching or listening at home – and still being able to find the right words to describe the action? If you can, maybe you could be a commentator!

GETTING THERE

If you want to be a commentator, you'll need to:

⚽ Be very good with words and have excellent control of your voice. Make sure you never sound boring, while also not going over the top and being annoying or distracting.

⚽ Be able to think quickly on your feet if something unexpected happens. You need to keep your calm in very high-pressure situations.

⚽ Remember that the match is the star. Especially if you're on TV – the commentator is just that extra flavour, the icing on the cake.

FIRST STEPS

Record yourself commentating on a full 90-minute game. It's a challenge! Do it as many times as you can, until you're happy with it.

Listen to how other people commentate and see if there's a style that you like. How will you react to a goal being scored? Will you be one of the calmer commentators? Or will you be like the South Americans, who are well known for shouting, 'Gooooooooool!' for several seconds?

Put yourself out there. A lower-league club might let you commentate on them. With your parent's or guardian's help, you could create your own website or blog, so people can hear what you do. Look out for competitions like Young Commentator of the Year, too.

FOOTBALLER

Alessia Russo

Alessia is one of the most recognisable players in world football. She's already played for Arsenal and Manchester United, and scored iconic goals to help the England Lionesses make history by winning the Euros, while also playing in the Champions League and a World Cup final. Alessia explains what it takes to be an elite footballer.

13

FOOTBALLER

ALESSIA RUSSO

Has the nickname 'Lessi' after her idol Messi!

Was part of the Lionesses team that won the Euros at Wembley

Holds the record for the quickest hat-trick scored by an England player (11 minutes)

'I WANT EVERY GIRL TO FEEL LIKE FOOTBALL'S A PLACE FOR THEM, WHETHER THEY WANT TO COACH, PLAY OR REFEREE.'

INTERVIEW

What drew you to football?

My brothers Luca and Georgio are a few years older than me. I remember when I was about four, and they were eight or nine, they would be playing games and training most days. I just did everything they did! They usually stuck me in goal and kicked balls at me for target practice! I'm a bit surprised I didn't make it as a goalkeeper!

I then played in a boys' team until I was about nine, when I joined Charlton's Academy, before being scouted to train with Chelsea.

How did you start your career as a footballer?

I decided to go to university in North Carolina, USA. I went there when I was eighteen years old. I came home because of Covid and when I was back in the UK, my brother Luca, who is now my agent, told me that Manchester United were interested in signing me. I couldn't believe it, as I was a big United fan growing up. It was a pretty easy decision to sign for them!

Who have been your role models growing up?

Some people think I wear the number 23 shirt because it was David Beckham's number, but it's the number of Chicago Bulls basketball icon Michael Jordan. His Netflix documentary *The Last Dance* was incredible! It's about how he and his Bulls team experienced the highs and lows of playing in the biggest games against the best teams.

Do you have any rituals that you like to perform?

I have an ice bath the day before games. It's cold but worth it! I have the same playlist of songs I like listening to, and just before kick-off I jump precisely seven times – it's worked for me so far!

Can you share some challenges you've faced in your career and how you've overcome them?

Playing in a World Cup final for England was something I always dreamed of as a kid. Not winning in the final versus Spain was really tough. I'll use it as fuel to make me even more determined to train hard, improve and be the best player I can be for when I get another opportunity to play in such a massive game.

What was it like to be in the Lionesses' squad when you won the Euros and got to the World Cup final?

The Lionesses are an incredible bunch of super-motivated, competitive players and we all demand really high standards from each other. You can also see, from the celebration pictures and videos when we won the Euros, how strong and connected we are as a team. We know how to party and have fun together! We spend so long together – in hotels, training and games – and realise that when we go on to that pitch, we give it everything. Just like a family, we'll do anything for each other.

GETTING THERE

So many of us want to be a footballer. If you'd like to be one, here's Alessia's advice:

⚽ **Hard work. No one is born to be a professional footballer. It takes a huge amount of dedication and sacrifice. That means training when it's cold, wet and dark, and when all you want to do is watch TV or see your friends!**

⚽ **Mental toughness. There will be lots of rejections, setbacks and injuries along the way. The best players know how to handle problems and move on when things don't go to plan.**

⚽ **Remembering it's a team game. It's vital to be able to work as a team. That means building relationships with your teammates, and knowing how they move, think and act – it can be the difference between winning and losing a game.**

DISABILITY FOOTBALLER

James Blackwell

England Cerebral Palsy team

Almost a quarter of the population of the UK have a disability, but football is for everyone and there are some amazing opportunities to play the game you love – just ask James Blackwell.

JAMES BLACKWELL

Striker for the England Cerebral Palsy team

Played in front of 20,000 fans at the Paralympic Games in Brazil

Won a silver medal in the Cerebral Palsy European Championships

INTERVIEW

Can you tell us about the journey you have been on with your disbability?

I grew up in a very small village, between Bristol and Bath. I wasn't allowed to go to the primary school in my village because I had cerebral palsy, but then the law changed and I went to the school. I was probably the cleverest kid in the class, the best runner, the best footballer, but there was always that stigma.

I used to deny I had it. I wouldn't admit it to myself. Only my close friends and family knew I had cerebral palsy. You don't want to be seen as being different. In the end, I told people when I was twenty-seven. It was a massive weight off my shoulders. I was still James, still the same person, but it gave me a chance to say, 'I've got a disability and I don't care about it.'

How did you get to play football for England?

I was good at football at school, and I kept that going and played adult mainstream football to semi-pro level. Then, by chance, I found out about the England Cerebral Palsy team. I emailed the person who was running it and he said, 'If you've played to that level, we want you in!' So it went from there, and it's been a life-changing experience.

You're travelling the world, representing your country in front of thousands of fans – and you're playing football! Who wouldn't want that?! I train at St George's Park every month. To have that opportunity, with first-class facilities, is second to none.

What was it like going from mainstream football to disability football?

Being able to meet and train with people who have the same disability as me was massive. A lot of time when you're a disabled person, you feel isolated. But you are not alone. With the CP team, it was great to find that common ground. We've shared our life stories as a group – and there have been some tearful moments – but it has brought us closer together.

What advice do you have for a young person with a disability?

Don't let your disability stop you from doing things. Focus on what you are good at and work on what you can improve. In my case, it's my left side that's affected, so my parents made sure I got lots of physio on that side when I was younger.

I always say to any young person: embrace your disability; it is who you are, and it will give you resilience and make you stronger in later life.

DIFFERENCES BETWEEN CEREBRAL PALSY FOOTBALL VS MAINSTREAM FOOTBALL

7 PLAYERS PER TEAM	11 PLAYERS PER TEAM
THREE QUARTER OF THE SIZE OF A MAINSTREAM PITCH	MAINSTREAM PITCH
EACH HALF IS 30 MINUTES	EACH HALF IS 45 MINUTES

'OH NO' MOMENT

In 2015, I broke my neck. I was playing mainstream football and it was the first game of the season. I went up for a header, got fouled, landed on my neck and couldn't feel my arms and legs. We went to the hospital for an X-ray and the doctor said: 'I don't know how you're walking, because your spinal cord is severed and you have a broken neck.'

Bear in mind that when I was born, my parents were told I was never going to walk. There was a chance I'd never speak either. So I just took what the doctor said with the attitude that I've been told I'm not going to walk before . . . I will fight back – I will come back from this, just like I have done before. I was back playing again within six months.

GETTING THERE

If you have a disability and would like to follow in James's incredible footsteps, here's his advice:

 There are regional talent centres for players with specific disabilities, for example deaf or blind players, or amputee players, or cerebral palsy players. Meanwhile, at grassroots level, there are lots of clubs which have opened teams where players with different disabilities can play together – so you're with like-minded people who will understand you. And then there are the professional clubs. A lot of them have their own disability teams that are run through their foundations, plus the Premier League organise Disability Football Festivals. There are so many opportunities out there now, and it's only getting bigger.

REFEREE

Chris Kavanagh

**Premier League
Match Official**

What's it like being a top referee – right in the middle of the action?

> **'WE'RE LIKE CONDUCTORS, JUST THERE TO FACILITATE THE PLAYERS PLAYING TO THEIR BEST.'**

15

REFEREE

CHRIS KAVANAGH

First football memory is Gazza (Paul Gascoigne) scoring for England vs Scotland in Euro 1996

Refereed his first Premier League game in 2017

Previous job was recruiting and training referees

INTERVIEW

You are one of the BEST referees in the world. How did your journey begin?

I was thirteen, playing grassroots football in Greater Manchester. My manager took me aside one day and said: 'Your feet don't work as fast as your mind.' He meant I could read a game of football but my feet didn't have the same skills.

He told me there was a referee course coming up locally and he suggested I give it a go. That was a breakthrough for me.

What's it like being out there in a massive game?

The Premier League is the best league in the world, so to be on that pitch is special. Most of the time you're so focused on the game that you don't have time to take everything in, but you're always aware that you're in a really privileged position to be part of it. Overall, I love being a referee. It's a fantastic job.

How do you keep your composure when everything is happening so quickly?

Over time you learn how to slow it down in your mind. So, although everything's going at a hundred miles per hour, you've conditioned yourself to take your time, to think ahead and read what's about to happen. If you don't, the game will run away from you.

How do you get on with the players?

We have a much better relationship with the players these days and there's more respect in the game. The opportunity to talk to a player on the pitch and understand what they're going through is really important, and building a relationship with them off the pitch helps too. We understand how much pressure they're under, and likewise, I think they understand where we're at.

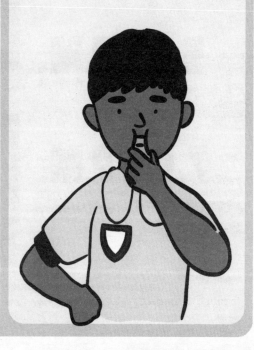

HERE'S CHRIS'S SCHEDULE FOR A BIG LIVE TV MATCH ON A SATURDAY, KICKING OFF AT 5.30 P.M.:

1.30 P.M.
Meet at the match-day hotel for a team talk with the assistant refs and fourth official.

3 P.M.
Arrive at the stadium. Goal-line technology check. Communication-kit check. Safety briefing with head of security and police.

4.15 P.M.
Team sheets arrive.

4.30 P.M.
Speak to the managers; brief conversation about behaviour and timings.

5 P.M.
Warm-up.

5.22 P.M.
Walk out of the tunnel, line up with the players, handshakes.

5.30 P.M.
Kick-off.

7.30 P.M.
ESTIMATE
Final whistle.

7.45 P.M.
Sports massage to help with recovery.

8 P.M.
Debrief from Premier League delegate – an ex-manager or footballer – on how they saw the game.

IS IT FOR YOU?

It's the last minute of a match between Liverpool and Manchester United.

A player goes down, claiming a penalty, and 60,000 fans are screaming for a spot kick. The eyes of millions of people watching around the world are on you, and VAR is monitoring everything too.

Could you stay calm, block out all the noise, replay the action in your mind and come to the right decision?

GETTING THERE

Football needs referees. If you'd like to be one, here's Chris's advice:

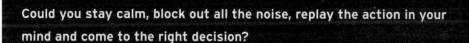 Contact your local county FA and see if you can join a referee course. They're good fun and the best way to learn.

Have an open mind. Don't be scared to go for it and give it everything you've got.

Don't be afraid to make unpopular decisions – that's the nature of the job. But refereeing is one big family and we have a support network to help you through difficult times.

Enjoy it! You're part of football, you're in the middle of that pitch – what could be better than that?

TEAM DOCTOR

Dr Kai Win

**Wolverhampton
Wanderers FC**

There are few more important roles in football than team doctor. Keeping the players safe, well and fit enough to play is vital to the game. That is the job of Dr Kai Win, who is the first team doctor at Wolverhampton Wanderers.

16

DR KAI WIN

TEAM DOCTOR

Born in Myanmar in Southeast Asia

Both her parents were doctors (it's in the family)

Worked at Birmingham City and with England disability teams

'IF YOU WANT IT, YOU HAVE TO GO AND PURSUE IT.'

INTERVIEW

What does a first team doctor do?

We look after the players' – and sometimes the coaches' – health and well-being. We help them to keep injury-free, fit and healthy, and performing at their highest level.

Players get ill just like we do, and it's my job to check them and make sure that they are fit to play. If there is an injury or illness, I look after them to make sure that they get better and can play again as quickly and safely as possible.

What makes a good doctor?

When I was younger, I used to think that being a good doctor was all about the knowledge – for example, all the potential reasons someone might be coughing. But actually, when you become a doctor, the knowledge is only a small part of what you need to do in your job. You have to able to communicate, understand other people and work within a team. Those skills, as well as empathy and compassion, are really important.

How did you get your chance?

I was training to be a doctor in England and I knew I wanted to work in football. I wrote a letter to Birmingham City and they replied, saying they needed someone to look after the academy players. I jumped on that.

You studied for 14 years in total – that's a huge commitment. What drives you to be a doctor?

I'm very compassionate, and I always want to care for and help others. That's how I see my life's purpose. It makes me happy every time I have a chance to make other people better, be that emotionally, physically or psychologically. Being there for other people – even just being able to make them smile – is what motivates me.

What are the differences between being a football team's doctor and a 'normal' doctor?

As a team's doctor, you feel you are part of the team and their journey, so you go through all the emotions of the season with them.

The safety and well-being of the players are always the priority, but we're also trying to improve their performance and help them be the best players they can be.

We also need a good relationship with the manager, as you make decisions together.

Also, football is a very fast-moving environment, so you need to have the flexibility to deal with whatever comes your way and think of lots of solutions.

BEST PART

When I was younger, we watched the Premier League so much and the players were my heroes. If I'd had a bad day or was feeling miserable, these teams and players inspired me and made me happy. So now I feel like my job is to be part of the team and make the players shine, so that they can go out and inspire other people.

HARDEST PART

As a football doctor,
the toughest part of the job is when someone
you are responsible for gets injured. Many times, my job
is to tell the coaches something negative, if a player is ill or
injured. Depending on the coach and player, there may be an
emotional reaction and you have to deal with it.

IS IT FOR YOU?

It's the week before a major cup final, and you have to tell the coach that their best player is injured and cannot play. How would you deliver that information?

GETTING THERE

⚽ If you want to be a first team doctor, you have to become a doctor first. That means you have to study very hard to get into medical school.

⚽ You need top grades in all your qualifications, especially in subjects like mathematics, English, physics, chemistry and biology, so . . . get studying!

THROW-IN COACH

Thomas Grønnemark

You're watching the biggest match in European club football – the Champions League final. The winning team uses a throw-in routine that you've personally created and taught the players. You are right at the heart of top-level football. Could there be anything better? That is the job of Thomas Grønnemark. He is a professional throw-in coach, and he works with some of the world's greatest teams and players. This is Thomas's story.

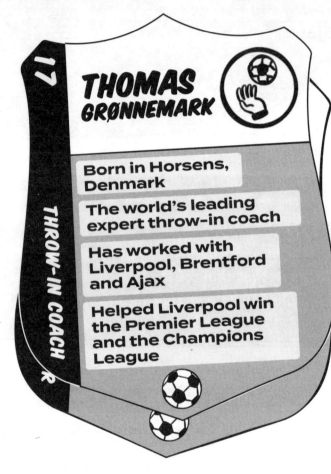

17

THROW-IN COACH

R

THOMAS GRØNNEMARK

- Born in Horsens, Denmark
- The world's leading expert throw-in coach
- Has worked with Liverpool, Brentford and Ajax
- Helped Liverpool win the Premier League and the Champions League

'I GET AS CLOSE AS YOU CAN BE WITH THE PROFESSIONALS . . . IT'S A GIGANTIC DREAM COME TRUE. SOMETIMES I HAVE TO PINCH MYSELF.'

INTERVIEW

How did you get this job?

When I was younger, my cousins could do really long throw-ins. I looked up to them and loved their throw-ins, so when I was a teenager, I started to try it myself. It became a really good weapon for me and my team, and I thought, *Can I teach other players to do it?*

I went down to my local library and tried to find a book about throw-ins but there were none. So I devised my own throw-in course. I began filming myself and trying different techniques – after six months, the course was ready.

I had the courage to ask a Danish Super League team if I could help them. Luckily, their head coach said yes and that was my way into professional football.

When did people start to notice your work?

One magic thing happened: I worked with a player in Denmark and improved his long throw-in from 24.25 m to 37.90 m – almost 14 m difference. Then he got a big move to Germany and, as a result, a huge newspaper asked to interview me. I said yes, knowing that many people were going to read it.

What was your big break?

In 2018 I had a call from Jürgen Klopp at Liverpool. It was perhaps the most important call in my life. He said: 'We had a fantastic season – we were fourth in the Premier League and we reached the Champions League final – but we were so bad at the throw-ins.'

He invited me to the Liverpool training ground the week after. It was just supposed to be a meeting, but he was so convinced about my knowledge that I got the chance to coach one of his players the very next day. The week after, we signed the contract.

How close to football do you get?

I work with the team and individual players, mostly in small groups and sometimes I get the whole squad at one time. I also analyse their games on the computer. It's a gigantic dream come true and I'm really happy that Jürgen Klopp took the step to call me. Many leaders and people with power aren't brave enough to give their power away.

CAREER HIGHLIGHT

Winning the Champions League and the Premier League with Liverpool. It was out of this world. Perhaps even bigger than the titles, though, was having the opportunity to do a job that had never been seen before – in the end, that might have been the most special.

GETTING THERE

Specialist coaches are a growing part of football. This means there is a real opportunity for you. You'll need to be:

 Creative and able to think in new ways

 Good at explaining things to others

 Confident enough to stand up in front of the team and teach them new skills

 Knowledgeable about how bodies work, so they can perform at their best

 Good with data so you can use the information to make important decisions around training and tactics

FIRST STEPS

Find the parts of football that you're good at or love the most (for example, running fast, free-kick techniques, kick-offs, throw-ins, goal kicks, corners).

Make up your own routines and training sessions to improve this part of the game.

Do you play for a team or follow a local side? Why not ask the coach if you can show the team the training routine you have created? You might be able to help the players get better.

LIKE THIS?
Check out the role of head coach on page 34 for a similar way into the game.

FOOTBALL FREESTYLER

Liv Cooke

If you think Messi and Ronaldo have got skills, wait until you see what Liv Cooke can do!

17

THROW-IN COACH

18

FOOTBALL FREESTYLER

LIV COOKE

Football Freestyle World Champion and record holder

Her online videos have over 2.5 billion views

Was on course to be a pro footballer before getting injured and discovering freestyle videos

'IT'S PRETTY CRAZY TO THINK THAT NO ONE HAS BETTER CONTROL OF A FOOTBALL THAN ME IN THE WHOLE WORLD.'

INTERVIEW

Tell us about your journey in football.

I grew up with two older brothers, and football was always a part of my life.

I was constantly playing with people stronger and quicker than me, so what I lacked in physical strength and height, I had to make up for in control and technical ability.

I played at the Blackburn Academy and learned so much there. They taught me how your mind will give up way before your body. When you think you can't run any more, you're probably only 10% done. You have to learn to control your mind.

At Blackburn, I was playing with a lot of the Lionesses you see now: Georgia Stanway, Keira Walsh, Ella Toone – that was all my age group. Georgia was always first into training and the last to leave, always running extra laps. That kind of determination was amazing to be around.

And then you got injured?

Yes, I seriously hurt my back and was completely out of all activity for about four months. But there was one thing I could do. If I was sitting down, in a certain position, I could kick a ball without pain. I started to watch videos of other skills I could do while sitting down. I didn't realise it at the time, but that was the beginning of my freestyle journey. By the time I was able to go back to football, I realised that I was more interested in being a freestyler.

How did you become the world's greatest?

I found out who was the best and worked out what she had that I lacked. For example, I watched a video where she walked out in front of 60,000 people and she was smiling. I was thinking that, in those circumstances, I'd have been a wreck. So, I needed her confidence. I kept putting myself in nerve-wracking situations to develop it. At some point I found myself at Wembley doing the half-time show in front of 90,000 people. I walked back into the changing room and thought, *You know what, I really enjoyed that.* That's when I realised I'd done it.

How hard is freestyling?

If you see someone else do a trick with a ball, you think it looks easy. But when you try it, you realise how hard it is. You could spend thousands of hours doing thousands of attempts to try to land that trick. And then when you do, that's just one in a thousand attempts. It's going to take another hundred thousand attempts to get to the point where you're doing it eight out of ten times. So, landing a trick is difficult, getting it consistent is super difficult and keeping it is an even greater challenge. That's why I train every day.

IS IT FOR YOU?

Liv's goal was to become the world champion football freestyler. To get there, she trained for six years to enable her to step onstage and control her nerves, so she could land every single trick perfectly. Could you do that?

You're also an incredible businesswoman. How did you make freestyling into a career?

I've always had a passion for business and there's absolutely nothing wrong with financial aspirations. You couldn't have a career as a freestyler 10 years ago, but now there are a lot of freestylers who earn even more than some footballers. Social media is a big element. For example, if a brand wanted to promote a new pair of trainers, they put a freestyler in them doing skills and that implies to the audience that those shoes are good for control or skills, maybe even specifically freestyle.

SUCCESS, THE LIV COOKE WAY . . .

These are Liv's tips to help you achieve your ambitions:

- **Do whatever it takes.**
- **If you want to emulate someone, write down all the skills they've got and practise each thing on the list until you've mastered it.**
- **And remember this: Excuses don't build empires.**

FIND IT ONLINE!

Search: 'Liv Cooke Ella Toone two touch' to see old teammates catching up over a kick-around.

LET'S GO

ESPORTS PLAYER

Tekkz

He's known as the Messi of EAFC, but how did Tekkz become known as one of the greatest esports players in the world?

TEKKZ

19

ESPORTS PLAYER

Real name is Donovan Hunt

Competes for Man City Esports team and records YouTube videos

Won 11 trophies

Represented England Esports since 2021

INTERVIEW

When did you decide you wanted to be an esports player?

All my mates would be playing outside in the summer holidays, but I was a bit of a geeky kid and I used to play FIFA all the time. I think I was in Year 10 or 11 at the time, and I beat one of the best players in the world. He was called Gorilla, and I also beat another called Tass. I told my mum, and she went online, looked into FIFA tournaments and entered me into one where the prize for the winner was something like £15. I won it and from then on started playing more and more tournaments – and here we are now.

Aren't your parents supposed to tell you to concentrate on your schoolwork?

Ha ha – yes, that's what my dad was like! He was the typical parent. But somehow my mum knew I was going to be a pro.

Was there a particular moment when you realised you could get right to the top in esports?

After winning that first tournament, I found more tournaments that the esports pros would enter and I'd have close games against them, sometimes winning.

So, going into my first ever professional tournament in Barcelona (FUT Champions Cup 1 on FIFA 18), no one really knew who I was because I'd just been playing all these guys online, but I knew I could win it. And I actually did win it!

What are the best bits of your life now, as a professional esports player?

You get to travel the world, playing FIFA tournaments. I've been to the USA, Singapore, Spain, Germany and Italy, so that's fun. My biggest highlights have been winning tournaments because it's such a good feeling –you're one of the best in the world. And meeting players, too. I've met Steven Gerrard, Phil Foden, Jack Grealish, Declan Rice, Bukayo Saka. These are the kinds of opportunities that come up.

You can be quite well paid, too, through views on YouTube and Twitch, as well as sponsorship deals and by winning tournaments. If you win a tournament you might get £50,000. If you win the World Cup you get £250,000.

How big a part do things like psychology, physio, fitness and nutrition play for you?

It's not a physical sport, so you don't really need physio, but psychology is one of the most important aspects, in my opinion. This is an individual game – you can't blame anyone else if you lose.

At my first tournament no one knew who I was so there was no added pressure on me to do well. I had no reputation. But as I've got older, I've felt more and more pressure every time I play because people are expecting me to do well.

The Man City Esports team has a psychologist and I have weekly meetings with her. The job can be lonely, so it's good to have someone to talk to.

I also try to be healthy. I used to go to tournaments and have sweets for breakfast, but now I have fruit to keep me going and keep my brain ticking.

CAREER HIGHLIGHT

Probably meeting Steven Gerrard. A month after my first tournament, I got to meet him and play football with him for a YouTube video. I'm a Liverpool fan and Gerrard was my hero. I've never been so nervous in my life.

GETTING THERE

Tekkz's guide to be becoming a top esports player:

⚽ Watch professionals play and learn what works best in the game.

⚽ Learn what the pros are doing and put it into your own game.

⚽ Learn skill moves. They are one of the best things in FIFA and what separates great players from good players.

⚽ If you want to get signed by a team, you need to have a CV, and you get that by placing well at tournaments.

⚽ Build a name for yourself at tournaments to help you get noticed.

● ● ● FIND IT ONLINE! ✖

Check out Tekkz's YouTube channel for all his FIFA content, plus real-life videos and lots more awesome content!

LET'S GO

PSYCHOLOGIST

Dr Pippa Grange

A big part of helping footballers to play at their best on the pitch is about looking after their mental well-being. Sports psychologist Dr Pippa Grange is there to help athletes and teams overcome their fears and achieve their goals.

20

PSYCHOLOGIST

DR PIPPA GRANGE

Worked with England manager Gareth Southgate and with the women's team

Helped the England team get to the semi-finals of the 2018 World Cup

Is one of the main characters in the play *Dear England*

INTERVIEW

What does a psychologist do?

I'm a doctor that helps people to better understand their thoughts and feelings. That usually includes listening to the person, working out how they deal with situations and giving them the tools to better understand themselves. The aim can be for people to feel happier and more fulfilled in their life.

I became a sports psychologist because I thought it was really unfair how athletes are always only a mistake away from (sometimes very) public criticism. This made me want to help them deal with the good and the bad.

How did the job with the England team come about and what did you do?

The English Football Association had asked a recruitment company to do a worldwide search for the right person. They wanted somebody who worked on team culture and not just psychology, which I did. They had a list of over 230 people and after several interviews, they asked me to take on the role of 'Head of People and Team Development'.

It turns out that 70% of how we behave comes from the environments that we exist in. That means that to get the best out of people it's very important to develop an environment where they thrive. My job was to work on this.

I was part of a great team, including Dan Ashworth (who used to work at the Football Association) and Dave

Reddin, who had already put in place an excellent system, but there was a missing piece. That 'missing piece' was to create an environment to help players cope better as well as deal with and perform under pressurised situations like penalty shoot-outs. The idea was to create an environment where the players were better equipped to express themselves on and off the pitch.

Could it be YOU?

What skills are important when thinking of becoming a psychologist?

⚽ **Listening and observing. I'm constantly thinking about what I see and hear, and how I use those words and pictures when trying to help people. If someone is telling me what's troubling them, it's vital I'm hearing and picking up pieces of stories and memories that might be useful to better understand them.**

⚽ **Communication – my job means I will need to:**
- **Ask curious questions about a person's life.**
- **Explain complicated subjects (like why people are worried or fearful).**
- **Share my ideas in a way that is easy for the other person to understand.**

⚽ **Patience – things rarely happen quickly. It may be that as human beings we want quick results, but change isn't immediate and is likely to take time. It works both ways too. A psychologist will need to take time to understand the person they are trying to help, and it will always take time and effort for a person to understand themselves. This may mean working out a plan of action to change their mindset, their behaviours or the words they speak to themselves and to their friends and family. There is rarely a magical answer.**

CHIEF INTELLIGENCE OFFICER
Omar Chaudhuri

Numbers and data are so important for clubs and players. They help to show if a team is playing well, whether a player is training hard enough, or the chances of a club winning or losing a game. Omar uses numbers and maths to help players and clubs win more matches and trophies.

21

CHIEF INTELLIGENCE OFFICER

OMAR CHAUDHURI

Works with people who want to buy football clubs. He helps them work out which club to buy and how much to spend

Wrote a blog about why England aren't very good at winning World Cups!

INTERVIEW

What subjects are helpful for your job?

Maths, English and economics would be three important subjects. For example, I think English is important to tell stories, be persuasive and convince people of your point of view. And in terms of a subject I didn't study, I think a language like Spanish, French or Chinese, particularly in an industry like football, would have been helpful.

What were your first steps?

I decided to start a blog in 2004, when I was thirteen. I tried to use my maths skills to work out answers to questions I was reading about. Like, for example, did a referee give more penalties to Manchester United or Liverpool? Which club bought the best players each season? I used the numbers and data I found on the internet to work out answers to these questions and wrote about them on my blog.

What does a chief intelligence officer do?

I try to bring numbers to life. Presenting big tables of numbers can be quite boring, and no one is going to want to look at that for too long! So I tell stories: for example, why players shouldn't shoot too much from outside the penalty box or whether a short corner is better than a corner kicked into the box.

For shooting outside the penalty box, I worked out that only 3 shots out of a 100 are scored. However, 15 goals are scored from 100 shots taken inside the penalty area. This means a player is much less likely to score from outside the box. Managers may see my data and tell their players to only shoot from the best places inside the penalty box. My job is to look at the numbers and create a story to help people perform better on the pitch.

How do you stand out?

I would say by questioning everything. Don't assume that everything you hear or think is correct – instead, try to challenge yourself. Think about why you might be wrong and then see if you can find evidence to prove yourself right! Don't be afraid to try things and make mistakes too. I've written lots of silly things, but learned from them. If you never put yourself out there, then you'll never get anyone's thoughts, and you need other people's feedback to improve and be noticed.

Being involved in recommending high-profile managers to teams. It's a source of great pride. We helped Tottenham with Ange Postecoglou and the US women's national team with Emma Hayes. It's pretty awesome to help such major teams!

Could it be YOU?

If you'd love to work with numbers and data in football, you'll need to:

- ⚽ Have a thirst for football knowledge. It's vital to know the teams, players and managers – all the stats. Ask your parents to show you the EA FC Ultimate Team app.

- ⚽ Have a great eye for detail. Are you good at spotting spelling mistakes or a number in the wrong place?

- ⚽ Love numbers. If you enjoy maths, you'll have a great advantage when doing lots of sums and calculations!

- ⚽ Be good at explaining complicated things. Are you the one your friends go to, when they don't quite understand something? If so, this might be the job for you!

- ⚽ Be great at teamwork. I work closely with team owners, managers, coaches and scouts to help them understand how football data can be converted into practical ideas for them to use.

SPORTING DIRECTOR

Paul Mitchell

Paul Mitchell has worked with the biggest clubs and players on the planet. He's negotiated hundreds of millions' of pounds worth of transfers and is one of the most high-profile sporting directors in the football world.

22

SPORTING DIRECTOR

PAUL MITCHELL

Born in Manchester

Has worked with world-class players Sadio Mané and Son Heung-min

Used to play professionally for MK Dons before he got injured

INTERVIEW

What does a sporting director or a technical director actually do?

I look over all sporting aspects of the club, including player performance, academy player development, player and head coach recruitment, and a playing philosophy, as well as having the right physios, doctors and performance analysts. All those departments would then report to me and I would have overall responsibility for everything running smoothly.

How did you start and make that dream a reality?

I was about twenty-three and suffered a triple leg break on a cold wet afternoon at Notts County. That day set me on a very different career trajectory. As I was captain at the time of my injury, the MK Dons owner thought I could help around the club and he gave me the opportunity to work across every department.

Thankfully, the club also supported me to do my football coaching badges, which led me to help with coaching the first team.

What was your big break?

It was after I joined Southampton, when they were in the EFL Championship. The club gave me the chance to build the various sporting departments and then, six months later, we got promoted and I got the opportunity to work in the Premier League. Then the head coach Mauricio Pochettino went to Spurs, and we recruited Ronald Koeman as manager and brought in players like Sadio Mané, Dušan Tadić, Graziano Pellè, Ryan Bertrand and Toby Alderweireld. We delivered Southampton's best Premier League season, while being favourites at the start for relegation after the sales of many of the previous season's best players (Lallana, Shaw, Chambers, Lovren and Lambert).

Have you had a 'pinch yourself' moment?

It was probably when I joined Red Bull and I moved into my apartment in Leipzig, Germany. I realised it was a little bit out of my comfort zone and thought, *Wow, I've come a long way from MK Dons*, and I questioned myself: could I work abroad? I couldn't speak the language, but it ended up being a fantastic opportunity for me. I came from a council estate in Manchester and was travelling around the world to places like Brazil and the USA.

Have you had a player that has stood out?

I think there are two:

- **Sadio Mané. He is super humble and very respectful, with a huge work ethic. And from that first game at Southampton, he immediately rose to the challenge in one of the toughest leagues in the world.**
- **Harry Kane. It's his resilience, dedication and mindset. He went out on loan to multiple clubs, including Leyton Orient, Norwich and Leicester City, while having that rock-solid confidence that he could be an elite, international player. He was always the first in, last out of training and set the standards for the rest of the squad. If you want to paint the picture of the ultimate professional on and off the pitch, it would be Harry.**

And there are so many more players I could mention!

What sort of skills do you need to be a sporting director?

⚽ **Communication. You need to be good at speaking to the club's owners, your staff and, most importantly, the players.**

⚽ **Being authentic. It's difficult for people to trust you if you can't be relied upon to do what you say you'll do.**

⚽ **Being disciplined. In football there are so many distractions: the media, the volatility of results, travel time, multiple competitions, injuries, etc. As a leader in the club, you need to remain calm, level-headed and disciplined, as people look to you to set the highest standards.**

What advice would you give someone who wants to follow in your footsteps?

 Believe in yourself and believe in your journey. Don't rush through the learning cycle, because all the hours of work, good decisions, bad decisions, learnings, analysis and reflections are vital.

 Be patient. There's lots to learn and you can't jump the first few chapters of the book. Understand the basics and perfect them. The skills I learned along the way have just been so vital.

TIPS FROM THE TOP

'Get on mailing lists of the football newsletters that are out there (students often get them for free), listen to podcasts and see if you can find a sponsor for your own team.' **JONATHAN HILL - Former chief executive, Football Association of Ireland**

'You will learn far more from your mistakes than any of your successes. I've made plenty and am proud of them! If you're passionate about something, you will always find a way to make it a reality and then start working towards your next goal.' **VICKY GOMERSALL - presenter, Sky Sports**

'Football is a small industry. Find a way in at any level as soon as you leave school. Not only will it get you experience, but you'll meet people who could help you find your next opportunity.' **JERRY NEWMAN - chief digital and innovation officer, Paris Saint-Germain**

'I'm lucky enough to speak five languages which has been a massive help in building relationships with players and coaches of many nationalities. Learning another language will open up incredible opportunities for you in world football.' **XABIER DE BERISTAIN HUMPHREY - international sports lawyer**

'You will always be inspired by those working alongside you in this industry. Go for it! Unlock your future through sport.' **KATE THORNTON-BOUSFIELD - head of PE and achievement, Youth Sport Trust**

'I used to play professionally with West Brom. Now I'm a podiatrist, which means I'm a medical professional assessing and treating people's feet and lower limb. It's a great job for anyone interested in football (and feet in general!)' **KEVIN BRUCE - musculoskeletal podiatrist**

ADVICE FROM YOUR BIGGEST SUPPORTERS IN THE GAME

'I didn't even know sports marketing existed when I left school. Playing football at school is a great way to set yourself up for working in sports sponsorships as teamwork is key in our industry.' **JENNY MITTON - managing partner and women's sport lead, M&C Saatchi Sport & Entertainment**

'Put yourself out there. Be humble but be persistent. Credibility is currency. If you really want something, you have to make sure you tell people that's what you want.' **ALEX STONE - former FA & FIFA**

'You know you love football, so don't be afraid to show it. Be proud, be humble, ready to learn and ask questions! Most of all, enjoy!' **PETER DRURY - commentator, Sky Sports and NBC Sports**

'If you want to work in football, then make it happen. I saw a manager on TV being interviewed and I knew, "That's what I'm going to be." Five years later and I was managing full-time in non-league.' **CHRIS ROBINSON - scout, coach and former manager of Cheltenham Town**

'Your local County FA is a great place to start your career. We're involved in the game in so many ways and are always on the lookout for passionate and hard-working young people to join our team. Do get in contact - we'd love to hear from you.' **JEFF DAVIS - Kent County FA**

'The football industry is an exciting place to work and women are an important part of it. If you combine your ambition to work in football with a strong work ethic and supportive community, then anything is possible. Go for it!' **YVONNE HARRISON – chief executive, Women in Football**

'Get a mentor – someone who can support and challenge you. And be nice to everyone you meet because it's a small industry and they could be your employer or colleague one day.' **LES HOWIE – UEFA grassroots mentor**

'At TOCA Social, our whole business is inspired by the way that football gives people that chance to relax, play, eat and spend time together. The opportunities around this game are almost limitless.' **MELISSA HERMAN – vice president, global communications, TOCA Social and TOCA Soccer**

'Getting work experience is really helpful. It's a bit like training with the first team as an academy player. See if you and your school can organise some work experience in the football industry. It could be your first step on the ladder.' **EBERECHI EZE – Crystal Palace and England midfielder**

'I've been heavily involved in using football to change people's attitudes and behaviours related to climate change ... who'd have put those two things together? Yes, football REALLY can help save the planet – it's that powerful. And you have a role to play too!' **RICHARD HOLMES – football sustainability expert**

HALF-TIME
ENTERTAINMENT

LET'S LOOK AT THE BIGGER PICTURE AND MEET THE PEOPLE CAPTURING THE ICONIC MOMENTS AND MAKING FOOTBALL SUCH AN EXCITING SPORT TO WATCH AND PLAY.

AS THESE PEOPLE WILL SHOW YOU, THERE'S SO MUCH ROOM TO BE CREATIVE IN THIS SPORT.

FOOTBALL IMPRESSIONIST

Darren Farley

Have you ever made your mates laugh by doing an impression? Do you love football? Imagine putting the two together and making it your actual job!

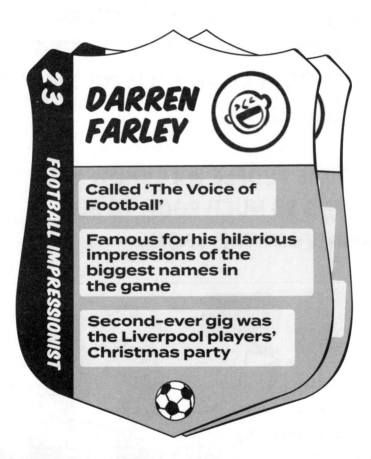

23

FOOTBALL IMPRESSIONIST

DARREN FARLEY

- Called 'The Voice of Football'
- Famous for his hilarious impressions of the biggest names in the game
- Second-ever gig was the Liverpool players' Christmas party

'I TOLD MY MUM I FELT LIKE I WAS DESTINED TO DO SOMETHING DIFFERENT, SOMETHING LIKE ACTING. AT THAT TIME, I DIDN'T EVEN KNOW WHAT AN IMPRESSIONIST WAS.'

INTERVIEW

What a unique job! How did it all happen?

In school I did impressions of teachers and my friends. I was obsessed with football, so it just became a natural thing to start doing managers.

In terms of a big break, a friend of mine put a video of me doing impressions on YouTube. All of sudden, boom! It went viral.

But I wouldn't say that video changed my life. I carried on doing a normal job, just putting up one video on YouTube every couple of months. Then I invested in a camera and started going out filming. My wife helped me. It was the best decision I ever made.

Day-to-day, what does a football impressionist do?

I have to be in front of the camera every day – filming and creating gives me a release. A lot of people go to the gym or do meditation, but for me it's being in front of the camera and being creative.

It's not just about doing the impressions, but also being able to create the content. A lot of time and work goes into scripting. I'll be sitting down, watching the Champions League, while writing two or three scripts at the same time because I've got so many ideas in my head.

I also do gigs around the country, so I'm on the road quite a lot. I love what I do.

Do you have to be responsible with your superpower? You can't just phone the bank pretending to be David Beckham . . .

Ha ha – you are tempted sometimes. I went to an event once and a very famous guy got me to ring his wife and pretend to be him. He told me what to say – and she went for it. It was one of the funniest things. I'm so devastated it wasn't filmed. A couple of times I've been to drive-thru McDonald's with the kids and ordered stuff as Steven Gerrard. They love that. You can have a bit of fun with it.

What impression do you get asked to do the most?

That's such a tough question, because it's different wherever you go. If I go to Scotland, they love Brendan Rodgers. In Liverpool, Steven Gerrard is massive. In London, people love Frank Lampard and Mikel Arteta, but they're not anywhere near my best ones. A lot of Liverpool fans love the Sean Dyche impression because he's the Everton manager and it's poking fun at Everton, so that's kind of how it works. It's so tribal.

As you say, there's an element of mickey-taking. Do all the players and managers like it?

I imagine they don't all love their impressions, and I've heard on the grapevine that there are a couple who aren't quite so into it, which is OK. But I've been lucky – the people I've met have all been brilliant. I even took Aston Villa training with Steve Bruce as another Steve Bruce. He was fantastic.

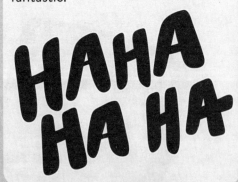

GETTING THERE

If you'd like to be a football impressionist, here's Darren's advice:

⚽ Be obsessed with people – the way they work, their mannerisms, the way they speak and look.

⚽ Put yourself in a front of a camera and experiment. It will grow your confidence.

⚽ Work at it. I'm grateful that I took my time and didn't go for it straight away, because I look back now and there was a lot of work that still needed to be done.

⚽ You've got to be funny! And keep your content topical and relevant.

⚽ There will be setbacks. The way the world is with social media, you might get a bit of negative feedback from people. But don't worry about that – it's character-building. The important thing is not to give up.

⚽ If it makes you happy and you work at it, you'll be absolutely fine. You can definitely do what I do. But at the same time, you'll be a rival of mine, so don't be that good!

● ● ● FIND IT ONLINE! ✕

Search: 'Darren Farley a few football impressions' - and try not to laugh!

LET'S GO

SPORTS PHOTOGRAPHER

Lynne Cameron

As football fans, we dream of being on the inside, of making friends with the players and being trusted by the manager. Lynne Cameron's job lets her do exactly that.

23 FOOTBALL IMPRESSIONIST

24 SPORTS PHOTOGRAPHER

LYNNE CAMERON

Started watching football as a kid in Scotland with her grandad

Has worked with Rangers, Man City and Man United

Was team photographer for the Lionesses

INTERVIEW

Can you tell us about your job and how you got into it?

I work with clubs and high-performance teams. My job is to capture the story of a sporting event in pictures. I got into photography originally because my dad had a camera, and I started taking pictures at school events. I also had a passion for sport and I remember thinking, *Oh, this is what the photographers do at the side of* the pitch during football matches – and that's how the pictures get in the newspaper! It was a light-bulb moment.

For me, it's the best job in the world. I love it.

What does a day in the life of a sports photographer consist of?

If you become a club photographer, these are the kinds of events you'll need to cover:

- Men's, women's and under 21's training sessions

- Press conferences

- Matches

- New signings

- Charity and community events with players, such as visits to hospitals and schools

How do you build a relationship with the players?

It's all about trust and connecting with people. If you do that, it comes through in the photography.

I was really lucky: I did a series with Steph Houghton when she was trying to get back from an injury to make the England squad for the Euros. Sadly, she just missed out. But she gave me access to everything. She basically told me to come around to her house, come to training – just take whatever I wanted and show her journey. Some of those images are so powerful because they show what athletes put themselves through on a daily basis for the chance of making it.

What are the highlights of your career?

The final of the women's Euros was definitely one. I've got so much love for the Lionesses. When you work with a team, you get a connection with them and you just want the best for them. I remember being on the pitch, looking around, thinking, *I've come from a small town in Scotland, and here I am.* There was a moment when Lucy Bronze – probably one of the best footballers that we've ever produced in the UK – was waiting to get her medal. Then she saw me and actually took the time to get off the podium and come over and give me a hug. That meant a lot.

With Manchester City, it was pretty special doing the Haaland signing.

He's a super guy – he's got such a great sense of humour.

Plus, I had the opportunity to be in Pep's office after a match to capture some photography in there. It was absolutely fascinating because he relived the whole match with his coaches. It's a privilege to see those things. And then there was the top-of-the-bus parade with the players after they won the treble. Capturing Jack Grealish just enjoying the evening after a long, hard season, singing and dancing with his teammates – that was special.

GETTING THERE

If you'd like to follow in Lynne's footsteps, this is her advice to you:

⚽ The best camera is the camera that you've got with you. I've covered Premier League games on my phone. It's about your eye: what do you see that's different from what everybody else sees?

⚽ Develop a style that's your own. Look at everybody's images and then pick the best bits and try to work them into your photography.

⚽ Work hard and be persistent. Reach out and ask photographers for help – if you get knocked back, pick yourself up and try again.

⚽ Be nice to everybody. The security guard is the guy who's going to let you run the length of the pitch to get the shot you need.

⚽ Get good at the social media side. Is there a burst of pictures that could form a GIF? Which picture would go best with that article? Video is obviously really important too.

⚽ Capture it all: the team sheet, the ground, your parking space, your cup of coffee – you're telling a story from your perspective and that is why people will hire you.

● ● ○ FIND IT ONLINE! ✖

Search: The Players' Tribune article: 'What it takes – by Steph Houghton' – you'll find Lynne's incredible photos of Steph's road back to fitness after injury.

LET'S GO

VIDEO GAME PRODUCER

John Shepherd

EA SPORTS FC

Millions of people around the world absolutely love playing football video games. Imagine leading the team that produces them . . .

24 SPORTS PHOTOGRAPHER

25 VIDEO GAME PRODUCER

JOHN SHEPHERD

Manages the production of the EA SPORTS FC video game

Used to work on the FIFA games, before they were rebranded to EAFC

Was inspired by Steve Jobs' speeches about the combination of technology and art at Apple

'I'LL ALWAYS REMEMBER WORKING ON MY FIRST FIFA GAME. SEEING EVERYBODY ENJOY IT WHEN IT WAS RELEASED WAS SUCH A HUGE RUSH. I REMEMBER DRIVING HOME, JUST BLARING THE MUSIC, THINKING, "I CAN'T BELIEVE THIS. WE DID IT. THIS IS SO AMAZING".'

INTERVIEW

What an amazing job! How did you get started?

As a kid, I'd draw the designs of a potential game that I wanted to create. I had the characters at the bottom and the little boxes at the top of the powers you'd have and enemies you'd meet. I was fascinated by games and how they were made – but I never thought that was going to be a career.

I also loved team sports, so those were my two worlds. When I went to a video game conference, I asked the people there: 'How do I get into this industry?'

As luck would have it, EA was hiring testers for a basketball video game, so I started testing that game and it all started from there.

So for your first job you got paid to play video games?

Yes! My friends used to make jokes when I went to see them after a work day, asking if I had saved the princess or not!

We were literally playing the game all day. We'd see if there were any issues or bugs, make sure the game was stable and give feedback on which areas were good or frustrating.

Tell us about your job now . . .

My responsibility is to oversee the delivery of the game each year, right from the earliest conceptual stages, all the way through to its release and the feedback from the fans.
So, on a weekly basis, I'll work with our design team to discuss new features; talk tech with the engineering team; try out new prototypes for graphics; look at the art team's new concepts and catch up with the operational leaders who keep me up to date on timelines and schedules.

As a producer, I work with lots of teams and it's important that I have a good base knowledge of all these roles. I'm a geek when it comes to technology and trying to understand what's happening in the industry so I can lead the vison for the game, both for now and the future.

Can you give us a couple of your pinch-me moments?

When we rebranded (from FIFA to EA SPORTS FC), we had the most amazing event in Amsterdam to reveal the game. It built up with Erling Haaland coming down the tunnel and it was an absolutely immense moment.

We had Ronaldinho there too. I remember him arriving with this group of people. Everyone was in awe when they saw him. We've also worked with lots of footballers over the years like Ronaldo to capture their movement in our game. So, it's pretty special.

GETTING THERE

If you'd like to work in the games industry, this is John's advice:

- Focus on your specific passion, whether it's programming, art, animation or design.

- Find opportunities to engage with the developer community. There are numerous events across the UK and internationally.

- Attend coding camps to study new technologies. It's also a chance to network with people in the industry and learn from their experience.

- Get help from your teachers and encourage your school to sign up to initiatives like Digital Schoolhouse (www.digitalschoolhouse.org.uk).

- Invite games publishers/developers to come to your school to give a talk.

- Events such as EGX, Guildford Games Festival and Develop Conference are a great place to meet people in the industry. They are always happy to chat to passionate gamers looking for an opportunity.

● ● ● FIND IT ONLINE! ✕

Search: 'EA SPORTS FC 24 | Official Reveal Livestream' to see the full launch event in Amsterdam. Haaland comes in at 32 minutes 45 seconds!

LET'S GO

CLUB SOCIAL MEDIA EXECUTIVE

Emma Coupar

Rangers FC

Social media is one of the main ways clubs stay in touch with their fans.

'I'M LIVING A LIFE THAT THE YOUNGER ME NEVER THOUGHT I'D BE ABLE TO.'

26

CLUB SOCIAL MEDIA EXECUTIVE

EMMA COUPAR

- Studied advertising and PR at college
- Set up her own digital marketing business
- Coached the girls' team at a secondary school

INTERVIEW

How would you describe your job?

I'm part of the social team who are responsible for planning and creating the photos and videos you see on Rangers' social media, such as behind-the-scenes sneak peeks or live coverage of matches. I'm a massive Rangers fan and I work for the club – it's as close to a dream job as you can get.

Tell us how you got there ...

When I was fourteen, my twin brothers played in a local youth team and I helped out at the club doing what I do now, covering matches and sending out tweets. It was very basic stuff and you'd be lucky if it was seen by 10 or 15 people, but it was great experience, which built up my skill set.

Then, after I'd been to university, Rangers put out an advert on Twitter for a social media executive and my brother sent it to me, saying, 'This has got you written all over it.' So, in a way, I've come full circle.

What's been your best moment?

The run-up to the Europa League final in 2022 against Frankfurt. I remember flying to Seville for the final on a plane full of people I look up to. It was surreal: *I'm 30,000 feet in the air, working for the club I love and speaking to Richard Gough –* *a Rangers icon – as we're on our way to a European final.*

How do you develop a good relationship with the players?

It's important for them to know you work for the club and you have their best interests at heart, because that trust shows in the content. When players are comfortable, they'll look for your camera, give a wave or add that extra little comment.

For example, when Danilo, a Brazilian player, signed from Feyenoord, I was there capturing the behind-the-scenes moments. He was saying how happy he was to be at the club, in his best Scottish accent, and waving at the camera. That kind of thing goes down so well with the fans, because he's not 'media Danilo', he's 'natural Danilo'. Sometimes you can even just give the player your phone and get them to film stuff – that's lovely content.

HERE ARE SOME OF EMMA'S KEY TIMELINE MOMENTS FOR A BIG OLD FIRM GAME AT IBROX AGAINST CELTIC WITH A 12 P.M. KICK-OFF:

9 A.M.
Arrive at Ibrox Stadium and put out a match-day post. Get content of the dressing room being set up.

9.30 A.M.
Team bus arrives. Capture footage of the players coming off the bus, walking into the ground.

11 A.M.
Share manager's pre-match interview on socials.

12 P.M.
Kick-off post. Minute-by-minute match updates.

2 P.M.
Final-whistle post. Put out the goals on the social channels. Reaction videos from the manager and players. Share any player/fan celebration content captured on mobile.

5 P.M.
GO HOME! And bring out my work laptop again!

GETTING THERE

If this sounds like your dream job, here are Emma's tips to follow in her footsteps:

⚽ Be passionate about the job.

⚽ Things will come in at the last minute, so you need to be able to think on your feet.

⚽ Attention to detail is important – you need to be a perfectionist. If there's a mistake in a web article, you've got to notice it, so good grammar and punctuation are crucial.

⚽ You're always on duty, even on a day off. If you get a text that something's happening, wherever you are, whatever you're doing, you drop everything to get that information out there.

⚽ Listen and learn from as many people as you can. There's always something you can learn from other people's experiences.

⚽ Don't wish for it, work for it – get stuck in.

⚽ Be mindful of who you're working for and the values they represent. It's not just about the followers, it's about putting out content that people really like and enjoy.

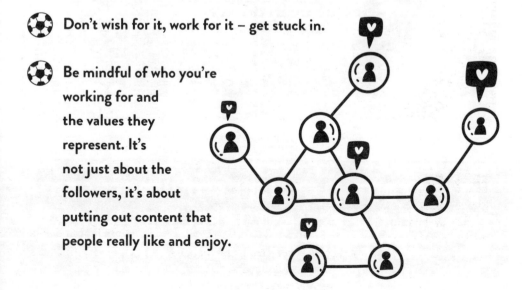

STREET ART INNOVATOR
Marc Silver

A picture is worth a thousand words. Imagine turning your love of football into art.

27

STREET ART INNOVATOR

MARC SILVER

Creates murals of legendary players around the biggest stadiums in the country

Has also created murals for Transformers and Dungeons & Dragons

Has even done a mural of Elton John!

'EVERY FOOTBALL CLUB'S GOT HEROES OF THE PAST AND THE PRESENT. I FEEL THE MURALS WE CREATE ARE LIKE MODERN STATUES.'

INTERVIEW

The people and brands you work with are amazing. How did this all start?

I'd wanted to be an artist since I was five, but I didn't know if I'd be able to make a good living from it. I ended up becoming a graphic designer and also worked in publishing. Then the real light-bulb moment was when I worked with a local street artist to design my son's bedroom to make it feel like the changing room at West Ham. When I saw what we had achieved in a small space, it showed the potential of bringing football street art into people's homes . . . and then the murals around the stadiums.

Your company did the famous mural of Jordan Henderson lifting the Premier League trophy near Anfield.

That season, it was clear that Liverpool were going to win the league. So I contacted one of the fan groups, Redmen TV, and I suggested my team and I paint a mural for everyone to enjoy. I went up to Liverpool and spent a day knocking at every single corner house that had a side wall which was the right size for us to paint on. Some of the residents were Everton fans so of course said no, but we eventually found the perfect spot.

We were ready to go on the night they won the league. My team and I were on a scissor lift next to the wall and the club photographer sent us the image of Jordan Henderson lifting the Premier League trophy.

The team worked through the night to get it done. The next morning, we were back there and Henderson came down to see it with his dad. He signed the wall too. These days, people do tours and have their photos taken with it. I'm very proud of that.

Does street art get the same respect as other art?

Some people used to dislike graffiti but now it's an accepted art form. We can thank the genius of people like Banksy for that. Steven Gerrard's reaction to the mural we created of him said it all. He said it was the most special moment in his career because it showed him what he had achieved and how he'd affected the lives of the community around him.

ANYTHING IS POSSIBLE NEVER STOP BELIEVING

GETTING THERE

Here are Marc's steps to becoming a street artist:

- Develop your artistic skills by drawing on a piece of paper over and over again. Practise is key.

- Get used to using different mediums, like charcoals, pastels, pens and pencils.

- Learn to use an airbrush. It's a small device which is similar to a spray can.

- There are people who do graffiti art workshops for children – check them out.

- Have a look to see if there's a legal wall space in your town or city. Underneath Waterloo Station in London, for example, you've got Leake Street Arches. You can watch the artists' skills and try to learn their process.

- To be a street artist, you've got to have a little bit of craziness about you because artists generally have that creative flair.

- Natural talent is important, but the most important things are patience and persistence. You're never going to get everything perfect first time.

- Keep pushing yourself to be better but learn to walk away when you can't do any more, and be proud of what you've achieved.

●● FIND IT ONLINE! ✖

There are lots of videos of the legendary players that MurWalls have turned into murals, including Aguero, Son and Saka, but make sure to search: 'A tribute to Elton John by MurWalls'. It's a great video and you can also see the grid system that the street artists use to create their design.

LET'S GO

PLAYER CARE PROFESSIONAL

Hugo Scheckter

Making sure that players are supported and well looked after is a massive part of football. It's one of the key responsibilities of a player care professional. Hugo Scheckter is an expert in this field . . .

28

PLAYER CARE PROFESSIONAL

HUGO SCHECKTER

- Grew up in the USA and the UK
- Got into football by playing Football Manager video games
- On the committee at Stonewall FC, the world's most successful LGBT+ football club

INTERVIEW

What does a player care professional do?

It's essentially everything that's not football- or medical-related. This includes helping players and their families to move house (and country!) or helping them to buy a car, learn a new language, set up bank accounts, acquire phones and pay bills. It can also involve helping to organise team travel and scheduling where the players should be on each day (i.e. training, a day off, a photo shoot, going to a school or hospital to see kids).

You might be on call 24/7 for any emergencies and urgent things that can't wait till the morning. Sometimes you just need to be at the end of the phone to talk to them when things are hard.

So how close do you get to the players? Do you become friends?

I think I got too friendly with the players when I was at Southampton, which can sometimes put you in a difficult situation if there is an issue between a player and the club, and you're caught in the middle.

When I went to West Ham, I made a conscious effort not to be friends with anyone from work until after I left. You can be friendly and very close, but never cross the boundary where you might be going to birthday parties or nights out or hanging out at their house. It's really hard to get that balance right, but important for people in my role.

The players must come to you with all kinds of problems and questions . . .

If it's important to the player, it should be important to me. If they're worrying about it the day before a game, then it's probably something we need to take care of.

For example, I worked with a player who didn't have a dining-room table for Christmas Day and his mother-in-law was coming over. He told me this at 10 p.m. on Christmas Eve. No shops were open, but we did it. We solved that problem. That's the kind of stuff that you might have to deal with. It is important for the player and their well-being, so you need to help them through that situation.

'OH NO' MOMENT

I once asked someone I worked with if they'd been involved in their car going missing. He couldn't believe I'd accused him of that and then the CCTV revealed he hadn't stolen the car. I still have bad dreams about that one.

CAREER HIGHLIGHT

Being on the bench for a Cup final at Wembley with Southampton – that was special.

Best part of the job?

I like working with people from all over the country and the world, and learning how to get the best out of them and help them.

Hardest part of the job?

The work–life balance. It's a 24/7 job, so trying to have time away from work is really tricky.

Have YOU got the SKILLS?

If you'd like to work in this highly important part of football, you'll need to be:

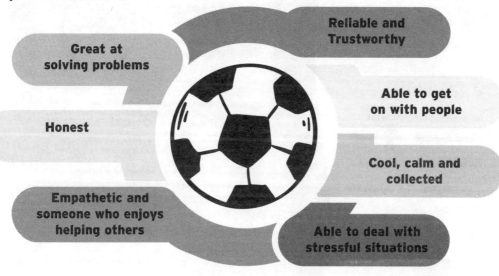

Great at solving problems

Reliable and Trustworthy

Honest

Able to get on with people

Empathetic and someone who enjoys helping others

Cool, calm and collected

Able to deal with stressful situations

GETTING THERE

⚽ At the beginning, you'll need to volunteer your time in football. Other experience will be helpful too: working in a shop, for example, will get you used to handling difficult situations, which will be really valuable.

⚽ Learning different languages will help, so you can talk to and understand players and their families from around the world.

PILOT
Louise Mack

Top footballers take a lot of flights. Whether it's a trip to a Champions League match with their club or a private jet that they hire themselves, flying is a big part of their lives. If you have sky-high ambition, perhaps you could be the one piloting the plane.

29

PILOT

LOUISE MACK

Grew up near Luton Airport and loved watching the planes

Has flown the Royal family, pop stars and LOTS of footballers

Her top flying speed is 500 mph

INTERVIEW

Amazing job! What's it like and did you always want to be a pilot?

Thanks. It's different to everyone else's jobs and I like the view from my office window! It's nice to be up above the clouds, seeing the scenery from up high. When I was at school, I always wanted to be a pilot but I never thought I could. I was actually told by my careers officer, 'Don't be silly, girls aren't pilots.' Thankfully, things have

changed now – there are more and more female pilots coming through, which is so good.

Which footballers have you flown?

I once took Thierry Henry and his wife over to Paris from London. They went into the centre of Paris to the Tommy Hilfiger flagship store, and they closed it just for him!

Then, a few years ago, we took the aircraft from Luton to Southampton to pick up a couple of people. We flew them to Italy, and then to Holland, and then took them back to Southampton. It turned out to be Virgil van Dijk and his wife.

I also remember, shortly before the Covid lockdown, we took Pierre-Emerick Aubameyang to Milan and that was all very last minute. It was in January, so maybe it was to discuss a transfer . . .

Which are the most luxurious planes?

A couple of sultans in the Middle East have their own Airbus A320s which are kitted out like hotel rooms. They are amazing. Generally, our aircraft tend to be slightly smaller.

MESSAGE FOR THE GIRLS

There's absolutely no difference between a man flying a plane and a woman doing it. If you want to be a pilot, just go and do it. Don't let anybody put you off.

What's been your proudest moment so far?

My first flight as a captain. It was also one of the most nerve-wracking moments, because the buck would have stopped with me if something had gone wrong.

Has anything ever gone wrong?

Probably the worst one I've had was when we had a problem with one of the instruments that tells us the airspeed of the plane. It made it look as though the aircraft didn't have any airspeed at all. My first officer's screen started showing some really weird things. It was a bit off-putting – especially as it happened at night – but we dealt with it.

To be a pilot, you'll need great problem-solving skills. You'll need to be able to read and interpret signals from the plane and from the people on it.

You might also have to deal with emergency situations, and act quickly and calmly to solve them. If you think you could do these things, maybe you could be a pilot . . .

As the captain, are you in charge of everything?

At the end of the day, the captain has to make the decisions and has the final say, but I would never ignore anything a first officer might say to me, even if they don't have much experience. I always say, if you see something, don't assume I've seen it – tell me. There's no such thing as a stupid question. It's very important to keep the lines of communication open.

GETTING THERE

⚽ Louise says that there are two subjects at school that will really help you if you'd like to be a pilot. The ground exams are the first phase of pilot training and they are all based around maths and science. So if you're good at those subjects it's a great start – and there are 14 ground exams you have to pass!

●●○ FIND IT ONLINE! ✕

Search: 'What's your in-flight entertainment? #LFC #Shorts' and you'll see how the Liverpool players keep themselves entertained on a flight!

LET'S GO

BROADCASTER AND JOURNALIST

Flo Lloyd-Hughes

Football fans don't just love watching the games; they also love to read, watch and listen to all things football on YouTube, podcasts, newspapers and websites.

30

BROADCASTER AND JOURNALIST

FLO LLOYD-HUGHES

Flo was brought up supporting QPR and then played for QPR!

Her family nicknamed her 'Gaz', after iconic players Gary Lineker and Paul Gascoigne

She has her own women's football podcast

INTERVIEW

What does a broadcast journalist actually do?

It's all about the words I speak and write! I work on TV, podcasts and radio, and for various websites and digital companies, talking (and typing!) about men's and women's football. I've also written a book!

So, how did you get into football as a fan?

I grew up with three brothers and

was obsessed with football! I played football in the garden with them all the time and had a subscription to *Match* magazine.

I went to my first QPR game when I was probably about six or seven. We've had season tickets and have sat in the same seats for almost 25 years now.

I remember crying all the way home after watching QPR lose to Cardiff in the 2003 play-off finals (it was a three-and-a-bit-hour drive, so a lot of tears!). I was so devastated about that result, and that's when I knew: wow, football was something I deeply cared about and it was going to be a big part of my life.

When did you think about becoming a broadcast journalist? How did it actually happen?

I wanted to be the first woman to manage QPR. I was so dedicated that for my oldest brother's twenty-first fancy-dress birthday party, I dressed up in a full QPR manager tracksuit!

I ended up doing a sports management degree at the University of Edinburgh and went to the USA for my study abroad year, where I was amazed at the US sports college system – how big it is there and how the media covered it in such a professional way. I worked for the university radio station, doing commentary on games and talk shows and writing for the online website. That's when I kind of fell in love with broadcast journalism. I thought, *OK, this is what I want to do. I want to talk and write about football.*

BIG BREAK!

I like to look at my life as football seasons rather than years! In the 2019 season, I got a message from the then-producer of the *Guardian* weekly podcast, which is a massive UK football podcast. He asked via X (formerly Twitter) whether I would come on and talk about the Women's World Cup.

That really set the wheels in motion for a completely different future for me.

Since June 2020 (when football started again after the Covid pandemic), the football schedule has been non-stop for me. I was covering three or four games in a week by the time football returned, and went from BBC London to working for TalkSPORT and writing for The Athletic.

Have YOU got the SKILLS?

What qualities do you need if you want to be a football journalist?

Confident in your opinions

A good listener

Brave and able to stand up for yourself

Resilient when faced with set-backs

Great at thinking on your feet

What's a mind-blowing part of your job?

I think working really closely with Ian Wright is one of the greatest things that's happened to me, but also just really having such an important ally fighting for you is something I never would have expected. He's just incredible and I'm so grateful to him for his support.

PERFORMANCE CHEF

Dan Sargeant

Just as racing drivers use the best fuel, elite footballers need the food that will help them perform their best.

30

JOURNALIST AND CASTER

31

DAN SARGEANT

Cooks for top players like Harry Kane, Jack Grealish and Connor Gallagher

Was inspired by cooking with his nan when growing up

Most popular dish is spaghetti bolognese

PERFORMANCE CHEF

INTERVIEW

What an interesting job! How did you get into it?

It started when I spoke to a player who needed help with his nutrition. Initially, I just outlined some recommendations but then he asked if I could prepare the food for him too. So we gave it a go. I started bringing all my ideas to life and it just went from there. Football is a very small community so if you're doing a good job, word spreads quite quickly.

Tell us about the work you do with players . . .

I use food for performance and medicine. Every player that comes to me is on their own journey, but mostly they just want to be better. My role is to give them the food they need to do that. We'll discuss how they're feeling, how they slept, how they felt in training . . .

A lot of it is about psychology and communication. For example, I might have a player who doesn't like fish, but if we have an agreed long-term goal, like lowering body-fat percentage, hopefully they'll be prepared to go with my advice and try new things.

What's it like working with players like Harry Kane, Jack Grealish and Conor Gallagher?

They're very driven and incredibly positive. Their mindset is infectious. When you meet an athlete who's at the top of their game, you want to be a part of that because they're winners, willing to do whatever they need to do to reach the top.

What's the best part of the job?

When I've put a lot of passion into creating a meal, used a load of vegetables and made it as nutritional as possible, and then I get a text message from a player saying, 'I really enjoyed that, can I have it again?' – that's a great moment for me. It's win-win.

DAY IN THE LIFE

4 A.M.

Head to my kitchen in Essex. Deliveries come in each morning, so everything is super fresh.

4.15 A.M. – 9.00 A.M.

Preparing the food. The kitchen is like a laboratory!

9 A.M. – 10 A.M.

Delivery drivers arrive, and everything gets packaged up and labelled. We have one driver who goes up to Manchester and one who goes down as far as Bournemouth. And normally I go into Central London to do the deliveries there.

12 P.M.

Back in the kitchen to start preparing for the following day. We do a lot of slow cooking, which breaks the food down more to make it easier to digest.

GETTING THERE

Dan's tips for how to eat to perform at your best:

⚽ Eat food that's as natural as possible. Anything that's come from the land, the ground or the sea. If it rots, that means it's natural and not full of preservatives.

⚽ Before a game, try eating any kind of dark red fruit like pomegranate, blueberry or beetroot. These have a nitrate which oxygenates the blood, giving you energy and supporting your immune system.

⚽ A few hours after a game, especially if you've been working hard, try eating pineapple. It contains bromelain, which has anti-inflammatory properties.

⚽ If you're injured, keep the carbs lower and the protein higher. Eggs are a good source of protein; you also want really good quality fats like nuts, avocados and seeds.

⚽ When you're playing, you're expending more energy, so you can up your carb intake with things like rice and pasta.

⚽ If you're feeling anxious, instead of eating sweets, try eating fruit or yoghurt with good bacteria in it. Food can make a big difference to your mental health.

If you want to work in football, you don't have to start at Premier League level. Look slightly lower down, prove yourself and grow that way.

To be a performance chef, you have to be passionate about nutrition and cooking, as well as inquisitive and creative to come up with new dishes – and always keep your finger on the pulse. This industry is constantly evolving because we're learning all the time about the effect that food can have on the body and mind.

'FOOD IS FUNDAMENTAL FOR PERFORMANCE AND RECOVERY. YOU COULD BE PERFORMING AT ONLY 80% OF WHAT YOU'RE CAPABLE OF AND NOT EVEN KNOW IT.'

DECLAN'S GAMEPLAN FOR SUCCESS!

Declan Rice is one of the top footballers in the world, but his journey has not always been straightforward – so how did he get there? His parents, Sean and Steph, share what it takes to build a career in the football industry.

BE FLEXIBLE AND WILLING TO LEARN NEW THINGS

Dec grew up playing central defence but developed into a defensive midfielder as he broke into West Ham's first team squad. The new position required a completely different skill set and Dec had to recreate himself. We had many conversations with him about what happened at the training ground each day, asking, 'What did you do well?' and 'What did you learn?'

He didn't shy away from talking about mistakes and weaknesses, because he had a thirst for knowledge and a desire to drive his performance levels higher and higher. See if you can be the same.

TRY TO SURROUND YOURSELF WITH GOOD PEOPLE AND BE A TEAM PLAYER

Dec always got on well with others, even his older brothers' friends, who he'd play football with all the time. He was five or six playing against fourteen year olds! Surrounding himself with better and older players is how Dec raised his game and developed his skills.

Fitting in was a huge deal when he was trying to break into the first team squad at West Ham. He needed to demonstrate lots of different qualities to be accepted by his teammates. It wasn't just about being a good player; it was also about being respectful with more experienced teammates.

Because of Dec's strong work ethic and his willingness to improve, he impressed those around him. In turn, they accepted him and made him feel part of the squad.

Be respectful to the people around you. They'll be more likely to help you to succeed.

BE FIRST IN AND LAST OUT!

Dec was obsessed with being early for training. He'd even want to put the cones out, get the ball bags ready and put the nets on the goals.

We'd sometimes be two hours early for training! If we were in traffic, he'd be pushing the back of our seat, saying, 'You're going too slow. I'm late.' We'd say, 'Training doesn't start for another hour and a half!'

If you can show this hunger in everything you do, people will notice and be impressed.

STICK WITH IT – EVEN WHEN TIMES ARE HARD

Dec left home at fourteen to be closer to West Ham's training ground. It was natural that any kid would struggle a bit and miss his family, and we'd say to him, 'It's your choice. If you want to come home, you can come home.' But Dec was determined and said, 'No, I'm going to stick with it.'

It won't always be easy. When it's tough, do your best to hang in there and ask your friends and family for support when you need it.

TALK THINGS THROUGH WITH THE PEOPLE YOU TRUST

Dec wasn't always the most skilful player in training, but we all worked together to help him improve. He'd come home and we'd lay out all the markers and cones in the garden. Dec would say, 'What do you think I could have done better?' or, 'What should I have done in this situation?' and we'd give him advice and talk it through. Then he'd get back to practising and working on what we'd discussed.

Always ask for advice when you don't know how to improve. Be open with the people you trust and they'll help you to work out how you can achieve your goals.

ENJOY THE JOURNEY

It felt like we spent half our lives taking Dec up and down the country for training and matches. It was tough for all of us and a big commitment. We had a lot of fun and would often cry with laughter on those car journeys, and we all knew every word to Elton John's songs, which were played on repeat in the car!

Those journeys were some of our best times together as a family.

You won't achieve everything you want straight away in football, but if you can enjoy the journey, you may well look back on it as your most favourite time of all.

KEEP REACHING HIGHER

Dec's first professional contract at West Ham was an enormous relief. We spoke to a football agent afterwards who said, 'It's not the first professional contract that you should be proud of, it's the second and third.' He was right, because you can't get complacent.

So when you start to make progress in football, don't think you've made it. Do the opposite: work even harder and be even hungrier to push yourself to the next level.

Good luck - all your hard work will be worth it.

TIPS FROM THE TOP

'It's an incredibly tough world to break into but if you want it enough and are prepared to put the passion and effort in, you can succeed.'
LIAM FISHER - head of talkSPORT

'The most important thing is that you never stop loving and enjoying football. Whether that be as a player, coach or club volunteer, work hard and BE THE BEST VERSION OF YOU!'
GARETH DAVIES - Elite Coach educator, Football Association of Wales

'One of the newer ways into football is through Talent Identification (scouting the players with the most potential). The FA offer a variety of courses and workshops, and you could try volunteering in your local non-league club to get a better understanding.' **RICHARD ALLEN, high performance specialist at FIFA and advisor at Yokohama FC**

'To me, teaching sport is the best job in the world. You're encouraging kids to enjoy it and you're right in the thick of it. It means every single morning you're getting up doing something you love.' **NOEL BRADBURY - deputy headteacher, St Gregory's Catholic School, Kent**

'It's such a fun and diverse industry, with a multitude of skill sets required so everyone can find a role that will suit their strengths. Find your thing and follow it!'
KATIE GRITT - head of marketing - Sport at Panini

ADVICE FROM YOUR BIGGEST SUPPORTERS IN THE GAME

'I teach yoga and meditation to footballers and I absolutely love it. It just shows there are so many different ways to get close to the game.' **CALLUM HOSIER – Holistic Hosier**

'As well as the 50 brilliant ways in this book, I'd say there are probably as many as 100 more different career options for you to explore within the football industry. So think about what your interests are and then spend some time researching the roles in football that really excite you.' **TOBY FRENCH – Careersinfootball.com Founder**

'Getting a job in the football industry is hard, but the toughest part is staying in it as there'll always be someone ready to take your place. You need commitment, focus, resilience, sacrifice and belief.' **ALEX LEVACK – football agent**

'My life journey started in the Ivory Coast and, through football, it has taken me to many places around the world. Wherever I go, people are playing and working in football. We need this diversity so, whoever you are, wherever you come from, there is a place for you in football.' **YAYA TOURÉ – ex-Manchester City and Ivory Coast footballer and manager**

'The game teaches us to keep going when things are tough. The combination of working hard and being resilient whilst still having fun is crucial. It's the winning formula.' **FREDDIE LJUNGBERG – ex-Arsenal and Sweden international footballer and media pundit**

'Playing football taught me to focus and I now use this skill working in the football industry. Keep learning, talk to people who love football too and read and watch everything you can about it.' **BEX SMITH – ex-New Zealand Champions League-winning captain, women's football consultant and media analyst**

'No matter what your skills, qualifications or experience, there are roles in football for you. You will have to work hard and sometimes work evenings and weekends but you'll get to meet incredible athletes and experience amazing atmospheres.' **ASHLEY HACKETT - chief executive, Blackpool Football Club Community Trust**

'Just find a way in - any way in. Then do the jobs other people don't want to do, do them well and people will notice and remember you for it.' **ANGUS MARTIN - expert in using football to help communities**

'Never take criticism from someone you wouldn't take advice from. Ignore these people and make sure you know your stuff whatever level you're at!' **LUCY WARD - broadcaster and former player**

'There'll be moments in your football journey that are amazing but also moments you will find extremely challenging. The key is to remain positive as you will learn so much about yourself.' **JENNIFER MILDENHALL - Emerging Talent Programme manager, Manchester United**

'Everything is preparation for the next thing. I have had a ton of different jobs and I've taken something good and useful from every single one of them. They are building blocks (even if it doesn't always feel like it!).' **NEIL ATKINSON - host, The Anfield Wrap**

BACK DOWN TO BUSINESS

IN FOOTBALL, YOU HAVE TO USE YOUR BRAIN AS WELL AS YOUR BODY. FOOTBALL IS WATCHED ALL OVER THE WORLD, BY BILLIONS OF PEOPLE WHO SPEND LOTS OF MONEY SUPPORTING THE TEAM THEY LOVE.

THERE ARE ALWAYS NEW OPPORTUNITIES TO GET A JOB IN THE GAME AND IF YOU WANT TO BE SUCCESSFUL OFF THE PITCH, YOU'LL WANT TO MEET THE STARS BEHIND THE STARS.

CHIEF EXECUTIVE

Paul Barber OBE

Brighton & Hove Albion FC

A chief executive is the person who runs the whole football club. Paul Barber is one of the best around.

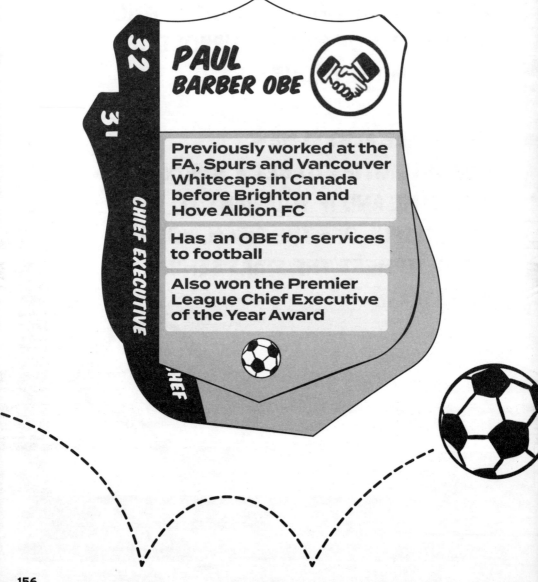

PAUL BARBER OBE

32

31

CHIEF EXECUTIVE

Previously worked at the FA, Spurs and Vancouver Whitecaps in Canada before Brighton and Hove Albion FC

Has an OBE for services to football

Also won the Premier League Chief Executive of the Year Award

INTERVIEW

Running a Premier League club is one of the ultimate roles in football. Can you tell us about your job?

My job is to do everything possible to help our teams win football matches. That means making sure all the different departments in the football club are operating at their top level, in order for those teams to have the best chance of success.

What ambitions are you working towards as a club?

Initially, when I joined, it was about establishing the club in the Championship. Then it was about getting to the Premier League and staying there.

After that we wanted to qualify for European football. And now it's about winning a trophy – being able to say for the first time in our history that we're the champions of something.

What does a day in the life of a Premier League CEO look like?

I like to run in the morning to clear my head and order my thoughts for the day. I usually arrive at the office around 8–8.30 a.m.

I start my day by meeting with the people in charge of the different departments in the club. After that, it could be a variety of things, for example:

- A press conference or an interview with a journalist
- Meetings with sponsors, the local authority or the police
- A Premier League meeting with all the chief executives of the other clubs
- Giving a talk at a company in a different industry to discuss high performance

Of course, the one thing we all look forward to and work towards is match day.

GETTING THERE

Paul's top tips for becoming chief executive of a professional football club:

⚽ Work as hard as you possibly can at school, because at a football club we'll need you to demonstrate all the academic and social skills that school teaches you.

⚽ I always find the best people that we hire are those who have been involved in football all their lives. So, get involved as much as possible. Play, help to organise matches, look after the dressing rooms, prepare the kit, help teachers with the coaching. Or if it's your local club, help them raise funds to get new kit or equipment. These things are open to everyone and they will set you on the path to working in football.

⚽ Always be willing to take on a new challenge. People who are prepared to say, 'Yep, that's not my job but I'll do it anyway,' or, 'I'll give that a go!' are always the most successful. I've benefitted from that over the course of my career. I wasn't ever the most talented, but I was the most determined.

⚽ Be the best you can be. Even when I cleaned cars as a kid to earn a bit of extra money, I wanted those cars to be the cleanest, so that my customer would come back and use my services again. Whatever you're doing, being the best you can be gives you the chance to get to the next level. And if you get to the next level, keep doing it, and so on. That work ethic is going to give you more opportunities than you ever thought possible.

INFLUENCER

Sam Miller

Sam is a football influencer. She posts everything to do with women's football on TikTok and Instagram, such as the matches she's gone to, the interviews with top stars, and lots of content she's worked on with the likes of the BBC, the Premier League, Google, Puma and EA Sports.

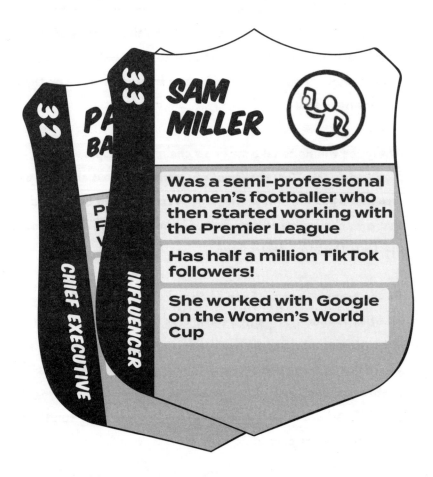

33

SAM MILLER

Was a semi-professional women's footballer who then started working with the Premier League

Has half a million TikTok followers!

She worked with Google on the Women's World Cup

INFLUENCER

32

CHIEF EXECUTIVE

INTERVIEW

What do you actually do?

I am a freelance content creator. I create content around women's football for my social media platforms, showcasing the women's game and giving people behind-the-scenes access. I worked with brands such as Puma and Visa, and I also have a partnership with Google Pixel and got to cover the Women's World Cup in Australia – I would use my phone to post content and advertise its features.

I've worked for UEFA on the Women's Euros and Champions League, too. I also work for broadcaster DAZN, talking about the different women's football leagues, and for EA Sports on their football tournaments.

How did you start off?

I was always looking for ways into football. I started asking for a job with a company making a women's football TV show. They needed 'runners', which are the people who do all the behind-the-scenes tasks for the show.

So, I started off as a runner, and then the BBC got in touch after hearing that I was doing a good job. I managed to work my way into football – journalism, broadcasting, commentating, social media and working with brands, which led to new introductions and connections at Facebook and the Premier League.

One job started a chain of opportunities!

How do you deal with things when they don't go your way?

I see lots of people feeling down when something has gone wrong with their work. A month later, they're still the same. Maybe it's a bit harsh but I think, *Move on, get on with it*, because what's the point of wasting energy, dwelling on something for so long. I got a massive rejection when I wanted to go to the 2019 World Cup, as the company wouldn't pay me to go. Instead of sulking, I channelled my frustration and energy into making something else happen. I emailed five other companies who needed help with their World Cup programmes and I made it to France!

'I THINK IF YOU DON'T HAVE THOSE REJECTIONS AND HARD TIMES, AND YOU DON'T HAVE TO WORK HARD FOR SOMETHING, THEN YOU PROBABLY DON'T TRULY APPRECIATE IT. FOR ME, IT'S ALWAYS MADE ME WORK HARDER AND KEPT ME MOTIVATED.'

Could YOU do it?

If you're thinking about being a football influencer, it's important for you to be:

⚽ Confident. You usually gain confidence from having lots of practice by speaking to friends and family about the matches, players, teams, the controversy and the special moments. So, talk about it all. The more you talk, the more articulate and comfortable you'll be in front of a camera.

⚽ Flexible. Social media changes a lot, with new apps and trends popping up often. Being flexible is about continuously learning, experimenting and finding new ways to understand what your audience wants.

⚽ Patient. No one can have millions of followers in a few weeks or months. You have to start small and build an audience. It can be a long and hard journey, but remember: great things take time!

FOOTBALL AGENT

Leon Angel

Do you fancy working on record-breaking transfer deals, meeting the top players and going to all the games? Then being a football agent could be for you!

33

34

INFLUENCER

FOOTBALL AGENT

LEON ANGEL

His favourite player was Spurs legend Jimmy Greeves – he even got to play against him in a charity football match!

Works with top players like James Maddison and represents managers like Arsène Wenger

INTERVIEW

What does a football agent do?

The role of a football agent has expanded over the years. It used to be about helping players with transfers and contract renegotiations. This has evolved into helping them with so many facets of their lives. For example, we negotiate boot deals with Adidas and Nike, or commercial deals with Panini or Football Manager.

We also don't just work with players. Often, clubs will ask us to help them find players and bring a deal together.

How did you start getting into the agency business?

I started out as an accountant and a client of mine was a sports agent. It all began with the transfer of Gary Pallister from Middlesbrough to Man United in 1989. A £2.3 million transfer was a lot of money back then! The agent asked me to help with the contract negotiation – and that's how it started. Gary asked me to look after him for the rest of his career and he recommended me to other players.

PROUDEST MOMENTS

Kyle Walker: We took him from Sheffield United to Tottenham but then he needed game time. He was on loan at QPR and then Aston Villa, and then made a huge impression at Spurs once his loan finished. He made it into the England team before becoming the most expensive full back in football history when he moved to Manchester City.

Eberechi Eze: He was rejected by numerous clubs, but my agents knew how good he was. We believed in him, and we managed to get him into the right environment at QPR. He lit up the team and got his move to Crystal Palace. We were so proud of him when he got his first England call-up.

Ange Postecoglou:
My co-founder Frank believed in Ange from the beginning. When I met him, I could see he was special. We were able to help guide and plan his career. After he managed the Australian national team, he went to Japan to coach Yokohama. He was there for three years, waiting for the right next opportunity. We told Celtic how good he was and he had a fantastic time up in Scotland. Then Spurs came calling. It's been a really exciting start for him.

Do you have a story that people wouldn't believe?

I actually have a story about the Pope, Arsène Wenger and Diego Maradona! Arsène had agreed to manage a team for a 'Peace Match' hosted by the Pope. It was on the same day as the transfer window closing, and a deal for a striker for Arsenal had fallen through. It turned out Arsène was keen on Danny Welbeck (who was at Manchester United at the time). We ended up having a private meeting with the Pope before the game, while I was on the phone, negotiating with Manchester United!

Maradona was in front of us in the queue, incredibly nervous to meet the Pope. I was more worried about trying to finish the deal!

What subjects at school are most useful for someone who wants to be a football agent?

I would say languages are important. I remember watching Arsène Wenger doing an interview a few years ago. The first question to him was in English, the second in French, the third in German and the fourth in Spanish. He answered each one in the language it was asked. There was then a question in Japanese and, although he understood it, he apologised and asked if he could answer in English! Being able to speak to players in their language is hugely helpful too.

GETTING THERE

There can be many different paths to becoming an agent. Here are a few routes that agents at Leon's agency have taken:

- ⚽ **University:** We have agents who have studied all kinds of subjects at university, such as geography or law. Most weren't sport-related courses.

- ⚽ **Recruiters:** Some people have a great ability to identify and find the best, next-generation footballers. We are given those recommendations, and we speak to the players and their parents to see if we can help.

- ⚽ **Other jobs:** We have plenty of people who were at other companies first. Some were at brands like Nike and others worked for companies in different industries. The skills you can get from those other jobs then come in very useful. Your first role doesn't need to be in football – mine certainly wasn't!

HEADHUNTER

Paul Nolan

How would you like to pick up the phone and offer someone their dream job in football?

PAUL NOLAN

35

HEADHUNTER

Finds the right people to fill the top jobs in the sports industry

From Liverpool, and a big Everton fan

Set up his own headhunting business in 2005

'IT'S SURREAL TO COME HOME, SWITCH ON SKY SPORTS NEWS AND SEE THE RECRUITMENT PROJECT WE'VE JUST COMPLETED BE THE "BREAKING NEWS".'

INTERVIEW

What does being a headhunter actually mean?

We place people in senior roles in the sports industry. For example, a club might come to us and say they need a new chief executive or an academy director. It's our job to find them the right person to fill that role.

So, you're like a transfer director for the sports industry?

Exactly. These sports clubs and organisations are big businesses. There's a lot more to them than what you see on the pitch. So, we find the talent for the business as a whole.

We've got long-standing relationships with clubs like Arsenal, Liverpool and the City Football Group, and we've worked with most of the other teams in the Premier League too. For example, we found the right person for the technical director role at Spurs and the sporting director role at Newcastle.

You headhunted Dan Ashworth for his previous job as sporting director at Newcastle – can you talk us through that process?

We were looking for someone who could build something – that was important to Newcastle – and Dan had a history of doing that at West Brom, the FA and with Brighton. His track record was absolutely perfect.

With the roles we're looking to fill, the best candidates are often already in a job and doing very well – which is why they are such strong contenders. We reach out to them, tell them about the position and explain why we think they'd be a great fit for it. We ask them if they'd be interested, and if they are, we start the process of recruiting

them. We keep their best interests at heart and consider how this new job might change their life; it might involve relocating to a different country, for example.

PROUDEST MOMENT

One of them was finding the chief executive for Billie Jean King's organisation. She's a former world number-one tennis player who won 39 Grand Slams, but it's what she's done for equality that has made such a difference. It was an honour to meet her and work with her.

What's the most important skill you need to become a headhunter?

You've got to have a fascination with people and understand what makes them tick. It sounds obvious but there are a lot of people who aren't actually interested in others.

But I am: I'm naturally curious – I ask people questions and try to find

out their story. It's how I relate to them. I've always been like that, and it probably goes back to where I come from. I grew up on an estate in Liverpool, where it was about survival and protection.

You needed to find a way to get on with everybody, otherwise life was really tough. So, I developed these strategies to relate to people. It turned out to be a skill set that's a key part of what I do now.

Could it be YOU?

If you'd like to be a headhunter, here are five things you'll need to be good at:

- ⚽ **Connecting with people.** Your contacts will be vital to connect you to the right candidate.

- ⚽ **Research.** Finding the right person from all the candidates out there.

- ⚽ **Communication.** You've got to be good at explaining things to people and making sure everyone is being updated during the recruitment process.

- ⚽ **Organisation.** If you're trying to fill lots of jobs at the same time, your organisational skills need to be on point.

- ⚽ **Persuasion.** Can you help the candidate to see the full potential of the opportunity you are offering them?

> 'DON'T BE AFRAID TO DREAM BIG. FIGURE OUT WHAT YOUR PASSION IS AND FOLLOW THAT. WHAT'S THE POINT OF HAVING A REALLY WELL-PAID JOB IF IT MAKES YOU MISERABLE?'

KIT DESIGNER

Bryony Coates

Imagine seeing the team you support playing in a kit you've designed . . .

'IT'S NOT JUST A KIT TO THE FANS. IT'S YOUR TEAM, YOUR LOVE.'

36

KIT DESIGNER

BRYONY COATES

From Burnley and is a season ticket holder

Has designed kits for Bournemouth, Everton, PSV, Spurs and Burnley!

Also designed kits for the national teams of England, Ghana and Italy

Has met Pelé!

INTERVIEW

Did you always want to be a kit designer?

I grew up loving art and sport. My brother and I used to draw football kits when we were kids – they were just doodles, really, and I never thought it could be my job. But as I got older, my love of both continued and so I chose art and PE for my A levels. I eventually did a masters in sportswear design, which was when the magic call happened. Someone from Puma called the course leader and asked, 'Do you know anyone who's into football?' And that's how it all started. I landed the job at Puma and went off to Germany to begin my career as a kit designer.

How does it feel, seeing the England players in a kit you've designed?

It feels amazing, but I actually get even more of a buzz seeing fans wearing it, because they're the people who've connected with it enough to go out and buy it. It reminds me of my brother getting his first kits. And, on a personal level, I worked on the kit that Burnley wore in the year we won the Championship. Seeing my boys in my gear, lifting a trophy . . . My dad turned around to me and said, 'You did it, kidda.' That was a very special moment.

A KIT'S JOURNEY

It takes 18 months before a kit is ready to hit the shops. Bryony takes you through the stages:

Start by discussing with the club what their aims for the next couple of years are.

Talk to the players and manager to get their input – for the players, it's their uniform.

Create some early design ideas to show the club and get feedback on them. Introduce ideas for the training apparel – these will be linked to the match-day kit designs, so it's a family of products.

After six months, everyone should be happy with the direction we're going in.

Get samples developed by testing out colours, fabrics and fit with different factories.

Receive the samples and show them to the club to check they like it!

Order the kits.

While the kits are being produced, you speak to the marketing team and discuss the ideas and stories which inspired the design - these will

be used in the marketing campaign to sell the kits.

The kits are shipped and delivered to the club and the shops.

The marketing campaign kicks in.

The players wear the kits, and the fans go out and buy them!

What did you say to Pelé when you met him?!

That was in Berlin, ahead of the 2006 World Cup, when I was working with Puma. I was introduced as 'Bryony, our northerner'! So, I was like, 'Hiya!' It was really nice. He was a lovely guy, very humble and easy to talk to. Then afterwards I was obviously straight on the phone to my family: 'Oh my God, Dad, Dad, look at this photo!'

GETTING THERE

Bryony's top tips for becoming a kit designer:

⚽ Think about the story behind your design. Why does it need to look that way?

⚽ If you can get into using computers, 3D design (what we call CLO) is the way forward in garments these days.

⚽ Keep playing sport, because you'll naturally think about how you feel in a kit, what's comfortable and how the kit is put together.

⚽ Keep in contact with people. You never know where your friends from school will end up and maybe you'll make opportunities for each other in the future.

● ● ○ FIND IT ONLINE! ✖

Search: 'AFC Bournemouth and Umbro: Let's get started' to see Umbro and AFC Bournemouth talking about their kit partnership – Bryony comes in at 1 minute 38 seconds.

LET'S GO

FOOTBALL LAWYER

Daniel Geey

Players and their agents need help from lawyers to negotiate transfers and brand deals with companies like Nike and Adidas. Lawyers also deal with problems on the pitch, like if a player gets a red card. Multimillion-pound transfers are Daniel's speciality.

37

FOOTBALL LAWYER

DANIEL GEEY

Born in Liverpool, 20 minutes away from Anfield, and a huge Liverpool fan!

Has worked with top footballers like Declan Rice and Ella Toone

One of the authors of this book!

INTERVIEW

What does a football lawyer do?

I negotiate the contracts when a player or manager wants to move clubs, or a brand wants them to be an ambassador (e.g. Nike or Cadbury). And I also help to negotiate the big deals, such as buying or selling a football club. I'm always there to help players when they run into a bit of trouble like a red card, speeding ticket or fine for turning up late to training!

How did you get started/make it happen?

I started out as a regular lawyer but knew I wanted to work in the football industry, so I began writing a football blog when I was twenty-three on my website (www. danielgeey.com). I read and then wrote about every football case involving players like Carlos Tevez, Luis Suárez, John Terry and Nicolas Anelka. Suárez, for example, bit three different players and was banned for many games.

What was your big break?

The BBC read my blog and asked whether I could go on the six o'clock news to talk about it. Then a few football agents and clubs phoned me up because they had seen me on TV!

Moment you wouldn't believe?

Getting a call from Ralf Rangnick on the morning when Manchester United wanted him as their manager! He needed my help to get his contract right so he could sign ASAP! It was crazy to think the manager for one of the top clubs in the world would sometimes call me on a Tuesday afternoon for a chat!

Hardest part of the job?

Football can be very pressurised and demanding. My family is very understanding! There was one time I took them to Spain for a holiday and as we landed, I got a message saying that I had to be back in London for a massive club takeover that I was negotiating. We booked the next flight home, and I was back at my desk within 24 hours!

I've negotiated transfers on a beach, using a napkin to draft the contract, and while on a boat in the middle of the ocean with bad phone reception!

BEST PART I've had some amazing experiences, including:

Hanging out in the players' lounge and meeting Man City players like Haaland and John Stones.

Negotiating a transfer from the Emirates Stadium and the Manchester United offices.

Being flown around the world to speak at football events at stadiums like Inter Miami or Atlético Madrid.

Getting signed 'thank you' shirts from Phil Foden, Jérémy Doku or Ella Toone.

Have YOU got the SKILLS?

To work as a lawyer, you'll need to be:

Good under pressure

Good at reading essays

Calm when dealing with difficult situations

Good at writing essays

Able to explain complicated things simply and clearly

Able to find creative solutions to problems

What's been the proudest moment of your career so far?

I helped Declan Rice with his record-breaking transfer to Arsenal. Once the deal was done, we had a photo shoot where he held up his new Arsenal shirt to the cameras. We then all went for lunch with Mikel Arteta!

Lioness and Arsenal star Lotte Wubben-Moy sent me a signed shirt and handwritten note, thanking me for my help. It's the little things that make a big difference.

What advice would you give someone who wants to follow in your footsteps?

As a kid, I obsessively read *Shoot* and *Match* football magazines. I memorised the commentary on goals, knew all the stats, played Championship Manager and could talk about football all day!

Read, watch and learn as much as you can about football. If you can do that, you're already on your way!

Emma Kernan-Staines

The Football Association

There are lots of powerful, high-profile people involved in football – and they need someone they can trust to work alongside them.

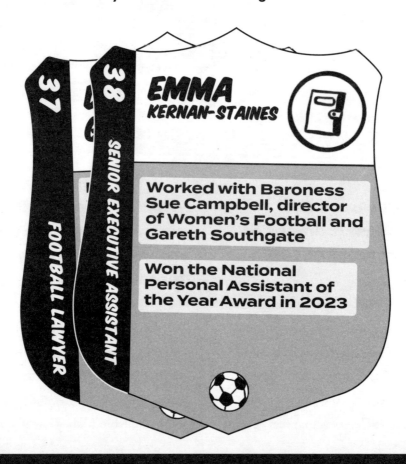

37 FOOTBALL LAWYER

38 SENIOR EXECUTIVE ASSISTANT

EMMA KERNAN-STAINES

Worked with Baroness Sue Campbell, director of Women's Football and Gareth Southgate

Won the National Personal Assistant of the Year Award in 2023

'I ENABLE PEOPLE TO BE THE BEST PERSON THEY CAN BE, AND THAT GIVES ME GREAT SATISFACTION.'

INTERVIEW

What does an executive assistant in the sports industry do?

My job is to help my boss be the most effective person they can be in their work, whether that's in a meeting, in front of the camera, in front of an audience or in an interview situation.

So, when working with Baroness Sue Campbell, my responsibilities have included ensuring that:

- Her schedule is organised, while prioritising the most important things
- She's got the paperwork, tickets, maps and files she needs
- The right people have had the chance to brief her
- She can get to places on time, in a non-stressful manner

I also filter all the requests that come in for work, interviews and meetings, and help to assess the priority of these against her workload.

Moreover, I encourage Sue to delegate work to other people. Everything comes back to how I can help her be at her most effective.

Those sound like really helpful skills in life, as well as work . . .

It's true. There's a lot about my job that I think helps me to be an effective mum as well. Similarly, it's a job which can lead to other incredible things career-wise. I have lots of friends who have been executive assistants and now have all kinds of jobs – chief of staff, chief executive of their own company, authors – there's such a big breadth of roles you can go on to do because the key skills in this job are so transferrable.

How do you balance helping other people with achieving your own ambitions?

As executive assistants, we are built to enable others. But I am also someone who will challenge and push back. I want to be listened to; I want to advise, because I think I can offer a really good opinion and I'm able to see the bigger picture.

What are some of the most thrilling things you've done in football?

When I was the executive assistant to Sir Trevor Brooking, the FA's director of football development, I used to work with the mascots, going on to the pitch with the England team, so that was pretty exciting. I was as close as you can possibly be to the players. We stood behind them on the pitch and felt that electricity in the stadium.

The launch of St George's Park, which is the national football centre and the home of the England teams, was also incredibly special. I'd been involved with it for many years and it was a long old journey. We were there in high-vis jackets and hard hats, up to our knees in mud, right the way through to helping to choose materials for the bedrooms, the carpets and everything else. Going there now, standing in the full-size indoor pitch, will never fail to give me a sense of pride.

I was there when it was opened by HRH Prince William and HRH Princess Catherine.

Were any players particularly nice?

I met Jill Scott recently, and she was incredible. What a lovely person – really down to earth, very funny, self-deprecating and absolutely exactly the same as you see on TV.

Could it be YOU?

If you like the sound of this job, these are the skills that Emma says you'll need:

- Really good communicator

- Top English language skills

- Loads of common sense

- Love keeping a secret – this job is built on trust

- Top-level emotional intelligence – able to pick your moment to discuss things

- Understanding human behaviour, psychology and team dynamics

- Always thinking about the people around you

If you have those things in abundance, you'll make a really exceptional executive assistant.

> 'WHEN YOU'RE LOOKING AFTER REALLY HIGH-LEVEL PEOPLE, IT'S IMPORTANT TO REMEMBER YOUR PLACE. YOU REPRESENT THEM IN MANY CONVERSATIONS AND SITUATIONS, BUT ALWAYS REMEMBER YOU ARE NOT ACTUALLY THEM.'

SPORTS BRAND EXECUTIVE

Juliet Aldersley

Off the pitch, players, clubs and managers are sponsored by a huge array of brands like Nike, LEGO and Panini. All those companies need to work out who to sponsor and how much to pay! Juliet has worked with the biggest clubs, players and companies in world football, and here she explains how it all works . . .

39

SPORTS BRAND EXECUTIVE

JULIET ALDERSLEY

She's worked with world-famous footballers like Reece James and Ella Toone

She also worked for Manchester City, Manchester United and Liverpool (controversial!)

She regularly does deals with LEGO, Capri Sun and EAFC!

INTERVIEW

How did it start?

I applied for loads of different internships and got one at Etihad Airways, in the marketing department. It was a three-month internship and Etihad were one of the major sponsors of Manchester City. I was going up to the stadiums to host employees of the sponsors at games.

What does an executive partnership do?

When I was at Liverpool FC, my job was to explain to a brand why they should sponsor the club. I was doing lots of research into the brand, like what kind of things they'd done before and who their target audience was. I'd then try to come up with a great set of reasons why the brand should work with the club.

What was your big break?

Accepting the role at a company called B-Engaged. My job is to work on all sponsorship deals with high-profile players.

B-Engaged's football squad is up there with the best agencies in the world.

They have Champions League winners like Reece James (England) and Kai Havertz (Germany), Alphonso Davies (Canada), Serge Gnabry (Germany). We also work closely with William Saliba (France), and England Lionesses Ella Toone and Nikita Parris. I have the responsibility of leading on all their sponsorships, which is exciting!

How close to football do you get?

I speak with the players, their agents and clubs every day! I try to help the players connect with the companies they want to work with, like Kai Havertz with Capri Sun or Alphonso Davies with Crocs.

What's the hardest or most challenging part?

Trying to keep everyone happy!

A player's schedule can be the hard part. They have to juggle training, travelling to games and having time with their families. Football is always the priority, and they need plenty of rest to prepare for what they do on the pitch, so it can be hard to find a moment with them. We need time to do photo shoots or record content for advertisements or plan their social media announcements. I have to 'manage expectations' (i.e. keep everyone happy!) between the players and the brands, so that everyone's satisfied.

'OH NO' MOMENT

Literally every day I probably have an 'oh no!' moment! It can be a real rollercoaster! It's how you get used to dealing with things when they don't always go to plan.

CAREER HIGHLIGHT

I worked on the Women's World Cup campaign, which was for LEGO stores all over the world. Being able to see the project come to life in the stores was special. The message was about inspiring young girls to do what they love and break down the barriers to play football – it was so empowering.

So what qualities are important to do really well at this job?

I would say being: 1) Flexible, adaptable and patient, as every deal is a rollercoaster! And 2) A good communicator, by being honest and straight-talking, as if something has gone wrong, sharing the problem with others can bring a solution that you didn't think of.

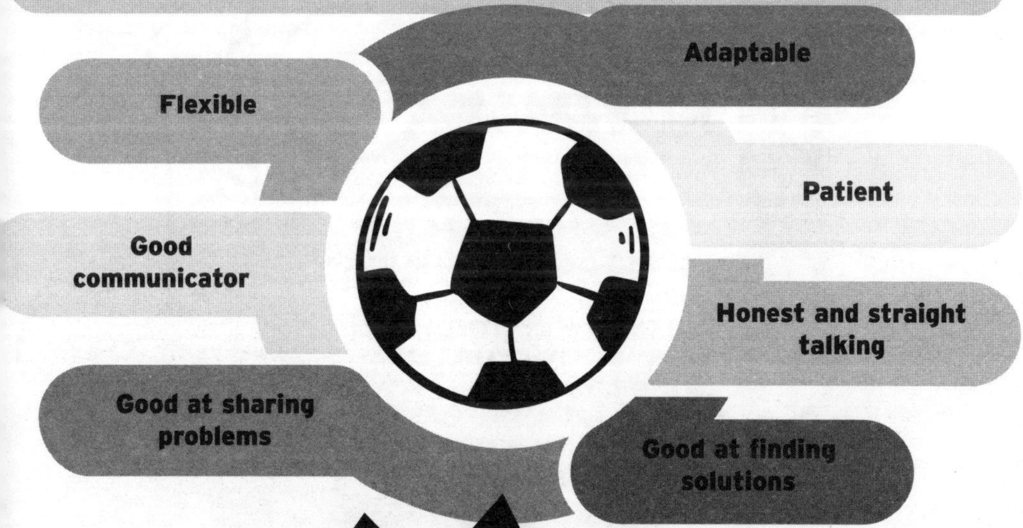

Adaptable

Flexible

Patient

Good communicator

Honest and straight talking

Good at sharing problems

Good at finding solutions

The best thing about the job?

The job is really rewarding, as so many players are inspirational. It could involve helping on a 'stop littering' campaign with Kai Havertz and Capri Sun or encouraging people to treat women equally. It's cool to be able to make a difference.

FOOTBALL INVESTOR

Kara Nortman

Having enough money to buy a football club is tough, but for football investors this is what their job is all about. Investors can come from the unlikeliest of places, including Hollywood stars, as Kara Nortman found out.

40

FOOTBALL INVESTOR

KARA NORTMAN

Founded Angel City FC in Los Angeles with Hollywood actor Natalie Portman and tech entrepreneur Julie Uhrman

Angel City's celebrity investors include musician Christina Aguilera and actress Jennifer Garner

ONE OF OUR ANGEL CITY FOUNDERS, NATALIE PORTMAN, SAID IT BEST:

'WATCHING MY SON AND SEEING HOW HE IDOLISED THESE FEMALE PLAYERS AT THE WORLD CUP WAS INCREDIBLE. TO HAVE THOSE WOMEN BE EXTRAORDINARY ON SUCH A GRAND STAGE . . . BECOMES CULTURE CHANGING.'

INTERVIEW

How and why did you become a football investor?

I first met the actor Natalie Portman through charity work we did together, when we were speaking about the US Women's National Soccer team's fight for equal pay. Natalie told me about her son's love of football and this gave us the idea to form our own team.

It was a huge opportunity to make a cultural shift in women's sports. I recruited Julie Uhrman, an entrepreneur and founder of a gaming console company, to join us and helped shape our 'female first strategy' for our soon-to-be launched Angel City FC. We wanted to bring on board a group of investors who shared our vision, including high-profile female athletes, entrepreneurs and entertainers. The aim continues to be to elevate women's football by creating a team built on a mission.

What is the aim for Angel City?

We want to have an environment where people have fun and enjoy watching female football players. We see the club as a platform for promoting gender equality and community engagement, as well as setting a new standard for what a sports team can achieve. One of the ways we do this is by asking that sponsors donate 10% of their sponsorship money towards supporting our local community.

This includes:

- **Delivering hundreds of thousands of meals to people who are housebound**

- **Football coaching, such as 'Footy Fridays' for girls who can't afford kit, transport and coaching**

- **Reading programmes for youth and female community leaders**

How can someone become an investor?

Buying a club isn't cheap and you need to find the right people to run the whole thing, such as sporting director, manager, sponsorships, community manager, ticketing and marketing. Lots of the roles you mention in this book!

Finding these people is expensive but, as an investor, I'm used to convincing people and companies to give me money to 'invest' in businesses that will hopefully make them a profit. Julie, Natalie and I made a strong business plan to show lots of investors just how profitable Angel City could be and it was a success. In our first season we sold nearly 16,000 season tickets and earnt $11 million in sponsorship deals!

Have YOU got the SKILLS?

What are some of the key skills you'd expect from an investor? Three important characteristics would include:

⚽ **Curiosity.** It's vital to be continuously learning and building knowledge to stay informed about the football industry. A successful investor is always curious and asks questions, in order to make the best decisions possible.

⚽ **Adaptability.** An investor is constantly making decisions. Sometimes it's being adaptable to see new opportunities before others do. It usually means being brave and flexible, and believing in yourself and your judgment.

⚽ **Building trust.** Life is about building relationships with people. In order to be an investor, people need to trust you and your business judgment. That comes by working alongside people over many years, so they believe you're going to do the best for them.

FIND IT ONLINE!

Search: 'Kara Nortman & Christen Press, Fortune MPW Summit 2023' to hear Kara talk about the success of Angel City and what's next for women's sport.

LET'S GO

FINANCIAL ADVISOR

Adam Osper

Some footballers are fortunate enough to earn lots of money. But since most players retire at the age of thirty-five, they need to know how to manage their money to live off that for the rest of their lives. That's where Adam steps in.

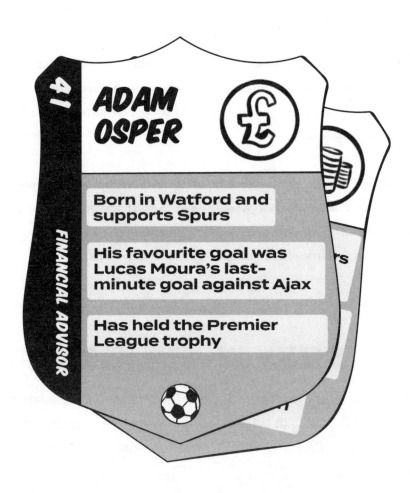

41

FINANCIAL ADVISOR

ADAM OSPER

- Born in Watford and supports Spurs
- His favourite goal was Lucas Moura's last-minute goal against Ajax
- Has held the Premier League trophy

INTERVIEW

What does a financial advisor do?

Imagine all the money you got for your birthday. There are always things you want to spend it on straight away, but your mum or dad might say, 'Why don't you save it for the future?' That's what I usually do. I say, 'Don't spend it now, put it in the bank and see how you can make more money.'

I'll plan with the player and their family so they can save money for buying a house, a car, or sending their kids to school or university. A financial advisor is someone who helps players to manage their money, just like a teacher helps you with your schoolwork.

How did you start getting into financial advice or sports financial planning?

I met Sam Sloma, who was an ex-footballer and is now a good friend. He knew lots of players so we would travel up and down the country on Friday nights to meet them at their hotels the night before their Saturday games. We would then sometimes go to the same nightclubs as the players and become friends. I remember the first big football player I worked with was Arsenal legend and French international World Cup winner Robert Pires. Working with him helped me because other players saw I was working with one of the biggest players in world football and wanted me as their financial advisor too.

How close to football do you get?

I'm often at club training grounds, players' houses or messaging them on WhatsApp!

I work with Man City player John Stones and he got me tickets for their final game of the season against Chelsea, where they were presented with the Premier League trophy! I ended up on the pitch with John and his family, and getting plenty of selfies with the players, the trophy and their medals. That was pretty cool!

What makes a good financial advisor?

Like in any job, you'll have to work hard and be dedicated. It's vital to get on well with people too. The players and their families need to trust you – that's because conversations about money can be difficult around what to save and what to spend. It is a big responsibility when players trust you with their money and their future.

'MY SECRET TO SUCCESS IS JUST WORK HARD, BE HONEST AND BE TRUTHFUL. DO THE BEST YOU CAN AND SEE WHERE IT TAKES YOU.'

Have YOU got the SKILLS?

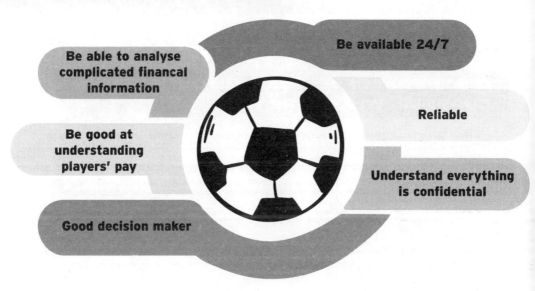

Be able to analyse complicated financial information

Be available 24/7

Reliable

Be good at understanding players' pay

Understand everything is confidential

Good decision maker

You need to know your numbers, understand what the footballers need and be a very good communicator. You'll be expected to:

- Be able to analyse complicated financial information and make good decisions based on it.

- Be available 24/7. If a player needs to ask you a question, it's important they can get hold of you.

- Be good at understanding how players get paid, how much they get paid and when they get their bonuses.

- Understand that everything a player says is confidential. Everyone wants to know how much a player earns, where they live or how much their house is worth. The most important thing is making sure all of this information remains confidential.

YOUR WAY INTO FOOTBALL: QUIZ

Not everyone can make it as a world-famous professional, but as this book has taught us, there are plenty of other jobs you can have in the football industry. Discover your dream football job by taking this career quiz.

QUESTIONS

IT'S THE DAY OF YOUR LOCAL YOUTH TEAM'S CUP FINAL. WHERE ARE YOU?

A With the rest of the fans, ready to cheer the team on and celebrate

B On the sidelines handing out water and orange slices so the team are prepared

C At the entrance, selling club merch and taking photos for their website

D At the scoreboard, getting ready to assist the other volunteers and help the game run smoothly

WHAT DO YOU DO WHEN SOMETHING GOES WRONG?

A I'm good at thinking on my feet and will come up with quick solutions

B I work best as part of a team so will speak to others to find a solution we all agree on

C I use it as an opportunity to change direction and do something creative

D I write down all the different ways to fix it and then decide which one is best

WHAT POSITION DO YOU PLAY?

A GOALKEEPER – I want to observe the game and organise my defence

B MIDFIELD – I like to be the engine room of the team

C STRIKER – I want to create attacking opportunities

D I don't play, I coach and support from the sidelines!

HOW DO YOU HANDLE HIGH-PRESSURE SITUATIONS?

A I thrive under pressure

B I get nervous but remember all the preparation I've done and push through it

C I tend to panic but always find a way to laugh my way through it

D I stay calm and keep my head in the game

HOW DO YOU INTERACT WITH THE REST OF THE TEAM?

A I'm the locker room joker; I've always got something to say

B I'm the one the team go to when they've had a hard day

C I have a few close friends but otherwise keep to myself

D I'm focused on the game and only want to talk strategy

YOUR FOOTBALL IDOL IS . . .

A MOHAMED SALAH – he's got the skill and the speed!

B JUDE BELLINGHAM – he's a great team player

C ERLING HAALAND – he's the best striker in the world!

D LIONEL MESSI – one of the greatest of all time

WHAT MAKES A TEAM SUCCESSFUL?

A Patience – you have to be ready for the right moment

B Teamwork – if you can't work together, you won't succeed

C Passion – you have to love the game with all your heart

D Practice, practice, practice – you've got to dedicate yourself to this game

YOUR TEAM WINS THE CUP FINAL! HOW DO YOU CELEBRATE?

(A) With a massive group hug!

(B) A meal with the team – celebrating together is what's important

(C) With a huge party! I'm ready to dance

(D) Celebrate? I'm preparing for the next season

ANSWERS

Mostly As

You could talk about football all day and you should! You know your stuff when it comes to the game and the world of football, and you're confident to talk to anyone and everyone about it. A career where you can use your voice, like being a stadium announcer or journalist, could be for you. Or even being off-screen as a stadium tour guide, head of community for a professional club or author might be more up your street.

Mostly Bs

You know how to get the best out of people and so a career working with the players would be perfect for you, whether you head down the medical route and become a physiotherapist or psychologist, or you use your skills to help the players in another way such as by being a coach, agent or chef.

Mostly Cs

Creativity is key for you and you shine best when you're channelling your passion for football into something inspiring. If you've got the creative flair then a career as a street artist, kit designer or documentary maker might be for you – or even finding your creativity in another way as a barber or video game producer.

Mostly Ds

You're a big picture thinker, and working out how to get the best outcome in any situation is what you do best. Whether you can imagine how to build a stadium like an architect, how to run it like a chief executive or how to negotiate the contracts like a lawyer, your way into football is all about helping the industry to work better and improve.

POST-MATCH INTERVIEWS

FOOTBALL NEVER STOPS AND NOR DO THE INCREDIBLE STORIES THAT SURROUND IT!

GET READY TO GO BEHIND THE CAMERA, IN TO THE STUDIO AND EVERYWHERE ELSE THAT FOOTBALL STORIES ARE TOLD TO MEET SOME OF THE MOST INTERESTING AND IMAGINATIVE PEOPLE IN THE GAME.

TRANSLATOR
Simonetta Italiano

There's nothing more exciting than when a top foreign player signs for your club – but who helps them learn the language?

41 FINANCIAL ADVISOR

42 TRANSLATOR

SIMONETTA ITALIANO

Teaches English to top players and managers, including Sandro Tonali and Carlo Ancelotti

Translates at press conferences and interviews

Taught Aaron Ramsey Italian when he moved to Juventus

'I HAVE THE BEST JOB IN THE WORLD. I MEET THE MOST INTERESTING PEOPLE AND I MAKE FRIENDS WITH MY STUDENTS. IT DOESN'T FEEL LIKE A JOB. IT FEELS LIKE FUN.'

INTERVIEW

Firstly, Carlo Ancelotti is one of the greatest managers of all time. What was it like working with him?

We immediately hit it off. He is a lovely guy, very calm and intelligent. I've worked with many managers because it's so important for them to learn the language as quickly as possible – even more so than the players.

Generally, they are very clever, motivated and hard-working. That's how they've got to that position. The manager I had the closest relationship with was Maurizio Sarri (the Italian coach who managed Chelsea). He even asked me to become a member of his staff. I sat behind the bench and really felt part of the team.

Do you have to teach your students about life in the UK, as well as the language?

That's a big part of my teaching. I have made a list of things that it's helpful to know. For example, in Italy, if you're asked whether you'd like some coffee and you don't want it, we just say no, but here one of the rules is never just say no. Always say, 'No, thanks.' It's a small thing but it's important to how people perceive you.

Often when young players come over, they need a lot of support, even if it's just someone they can talk to in their own language. Also, I might be there to help them open their first bank account or rent a house. As they need you a lot, you develop a close relationship.

IS IT FOR YOU?

If the manager can't speak English, you might need to deliver the team talk to the squad for them. Simonetta has had to do this on several occasions. Not only are you translating, but you'll also need the confidence to stand up in front of 25 people and inspire them with the words the manager has given you.

What do you do if you're in a press conference with a manager and you think what they are saying is a big mistake?

Firstly, I think it's important for a manager to speak in English, not in their own language – otherwise it seems disrespectful to the journalists and fans. I always help them to prepare; we'll have some predicted questions, which we think the journalists might ask, and we'll practise delivering the answers.

Generally, there are not many surprises – but I have nudged managers under the table if I think something's about to go wrong!

How do you go about teaching English to footballers – and who has been your best student?

As it happens, the players learn to communicate on the pitch with their teammates very quickly. Football itself is a universal language. So, it's being able to communicate off the pitch where we need to do the work.

I try to make the lessons fun because I need the players to look forward to them rather than dread them. The quickest anyone has learned English with me happened with Sandro Tonali. We had lessons every single day for an hour and a half, and within two weeks he could make himself understood. That was very unusual – he was amazing.

GETTING THERE

Obviously, for this job, languages are the key, so:

 Study languages at school and get as close to fluent as possible.

 Practise with friends and family who speak another language.

 Think about which languages will be particularly helpful in football – Simonetta is currently learning Spanish because so many players speak it.

 And remember, as well as being a way into football, languages are also a superpower for other areas of your life. Simonetta says: 'With languages, your experience of the world is completely different. It allows you to cross borders and opens so many doors.'

● ● ● FIND IT ONLINE!

Did you know that one of José Mourinho's first jobs in football was being a translator for legendary English coach Bobby Robson?

Search: 'José Mourinho Translating for Bobby Robson at Barcelona' to see him in action.

LET'S GO

BODYGUARD

RF

The world's top footballers are among the most famous people on the planet – so their safety and security need to be managed by elite professionals.

43

BODYGUARD

RF

- Was in the British Armed Forces, Parachute Regiment
- Protects the biggest stars of sport, media and entertainment . . .
- . . . We can't name them here because confidentiality is part of the job!

'NO ONE WILL EVER SEE 90% OF THE WORK YOU DO. IT MIGHT LOOK LIKE WE'RE JUST STANDING THERE, BUT IN REALITY WE'VE SPENT 10 HOURS PREPARING AND BEEN ON THE PHONE THROUGH THE NIGHT.'

INTERVIEW

We see bodyguards in the movies – is what you do anything like that?

Parts of what you see in the movies are very accurate and parts of it are a load of rubbish! Fundamentally, our job is to ensure the safety of an individual or a family. We see and hear everything, so it's all about trust. Your reputation is everything.

You must have seen some pretty amazing things!

It's true. I've met a lot of actors and musicians that you can think of – and lots of footballers too. You get to see and do things that you'd never normally have the opportunity to experience. I've dropped people off at the Oscars and FA Cup final and I've been there when a client has spent a million dollars in 20 minutes!

It's an interesting world and we're in a very fortunate position, but we've worked very hard to get here.

What would you say if Messi asked you to look after him?

The first thing I'd say is, 'Yes, we can.' Then I'd go away and think, *This is going to be a difficult one.*

That's the truth.

His security is really, really good. I've been seriously impressed with what I've seen. Go on YouTube and search: 'Messi security Inter Miami'. His security is an ex-Navy SEAL, but this is unlike anything I've seen before. He follows him everywhere. It's really good, top-level stuff.

CONFIDENTIAL

Do you ever get starstruck when working with these huge celebrities?

Our company motto is: 'Never above, never below, always side by side'. It doesn't matter where you come from or who you are – you're never above, or below, someone. We need to be on a level playing field with the people we look after. Yes, they may be world famous, but we're all just human beings doing the best we can in life.

Could it be YOU?

If this is a world you'd like to get into, here are some tips from RF to help guide you on your way:

- We tend to employ people from a military background. That discipline, work ethic, teamwork, fitness and reliability are all key. We are all medically trained too. To find out about careers in the military, visit your local Army Careers Centre. You can find which is the closest one to you on the Army website.

- After you leave the military, you'll need a Close Protection Licence, which includes training in conflict management, vehicle techniques, medical qualifications and kidnap for ransom situations.

- You have to be aware that life doesn't go according to the training manual. Even something as simple as taking a footballer from their house to a restaurant might become complicated. You've planned a certain route, but there's a traffic jam or accident. How do you navigate around that? What are plan B and plan C? Are you in communication with the restaurant? These seemingly small things are all key elements to the job.

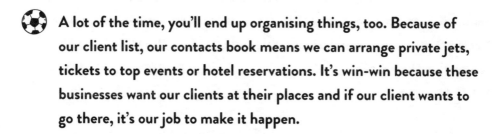 A lot of the time, you'll end up organising things, too. Because of our client list, our contacts book means we can arrange private jets, tickets to top events or hotel reservations. It's win-win because these businesses want our clients at their places and if our client wants to go there, it's our job to make it happen.

We have to be vigilant online too because footballers get a lot of hate on social media. If a striker misses an easy goal, they'll get lots of online abuse. We have to filter out the ranting from the credible threats to their safety.

It's a lot of hard work and there's a great responsibility but if you get to the top level, the money is really good. The day I left the military, I quadrupled my wage!

JOURNALIST

David Ornstein

David is one of the most famous football journalists in the world. He's been a journalist and broadcaster for the BBC, and he regularly interviews top footballers. He also wrote the BBC's 'transfer gossip' column. He now works for The Athletic and writes about top football teams like Manchester United, Arsenal and Liverpool, as well as players like Jude Bellingham, Mo Salah and Erling Haaland.

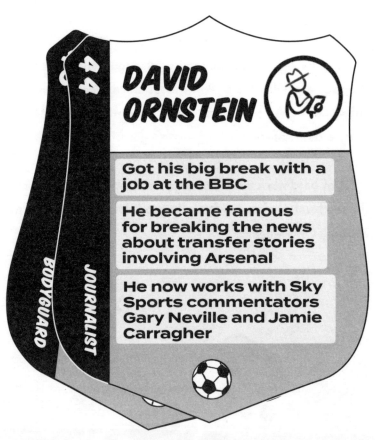

44

DAVID ORNSTEIN

BODYGUARD

JOURNALIST

Got his big break with a job at the BBC

He became famous for breaking the news about transfer stories involving Arsenal

He now works with Sky Sports commentators Gary Neville and Jamie Carragher

'LUCK IS ALWAYS INVOLVED TO GET THE JOB YOU ALWAYS DREAMED OF, BUT ONLY IF YOU PUT YOURSELF IN THE BEST POSITIONS FOR THAT LUCK TO OCCUR.'

INTERVIEW

What drew you to football?

I was totally obsessed with football while growing up. As a youngster, I was on trial at Chelsea but unfortunately wasn't quite good enough, so I started to consider how I could work in football in other ways. I thought that I could perhaps do that by writing and speaking about the game.

Growing up, I lived close to where the England team used to stay before games at Wembley Stadium. They all went to play golf when they weren't training. I would use my binoculars to see if they were about to start playing, and would then run on to the golf course and ask them whether I could caddy for them (which means hold their golf clubs as they went round the course!). I managed to caddy for Liverpool star Robbie Fowler, and Newcastle and Blackburn legend CBE Alan Shearer. I also got them and the rest of the squad to sign T-shirts and photographs! I made my own luck in managing to meet the England superstars. That's when I realised football was for me.

Have you had any setbacks in finding your dream job?

When I was at school, I wasn't very good at exams. Sometimes I panicked a bit; other times, I wasn't very good at working out how much time I had for each question, so had to rush at the end. Sometimes I just couldn't concentrate properly. It meant that for a while my exam results were not too great. I had to find a way to concentrate better, use a revision calendar to help me study and time my answers more precisely, so I could finish the exam.

Slowly but surely, I started improving, and persevering became my superpower.

BIG BREAK!

One of my first-ever stories was when I was still only doing work experience in 2005 at a local paper. I went to Southampton FC for a book launch for their striker Ricardo Fuller. I asked him a few questions when none of the other reporters were around and he said, 'I can be the best striker in the world, I can be better than Thierry Henry.' I went back and told the newspaper editor, who thought it was a great story to run. Their headline was 'Which Saints star thinks he's better than Thierry Henry?' The whole interview I had done was the main sports story in the newspaper the next day. I've never been so excited to see the paper in the shops. I had used my initiative and got a great story!

My big career break was when I moved with the BBC to their new offices in Manchester. The move gave me the opportunity to work on the radio (called Five Live); I also started writing for the BBC Sport website and was asked to be on the BBC News, reporting on all the different sports and football stories. I was getting such a variety of work through writing, speaking and broadcasting about football.

What qualities do you need if you want to be a sports journalist?

I can only tell you what worked well for me at the BBC: I just wanted to do as much as possible, so I'd get to the office early, at 6 a.m., to write the BBC transfer gossip column on the website. This meant I had time left in the day to work on the radio, the website and TV, plus going out to press conferences and interviewing people. I worked hard and took every opportunity.

The main qualities an aspiring journalist needs are hard work, dedication, initiative and being consistent – day in, day out.

POLICE OFFICER
Lizzie Lewandowski

Who has one of the most important jobs of all on match day? The police – and with people like Sergeant Lizzie Lewandowski around, we are in safe hands.

45

POLICE OFFICER

LIZZIE LEWANDOWSKI

Football Unit Sergeant from the West Midlands

Been in the police for 18 years

Travels to matches all over the world to keep fans safe

Manages dedicated football officers at all the West Midlands clubs

INTERVIEW

Can you tell us what you do as a football police sergeant?

I manage a team who deal with various issues around football, such as:

- Fights, riots, bullying and vandalism (hooliganism) on match days

- People running on the pitch

- **Looking after fans who need to know what pubs they can drink in and where to go before the match, to ensure they stay safe**

- **Racism, hate crimes, violence against women and girls**

- **Visiting schools to engage with young people, talking to them and trying to prevent them from becoming football hooligans**

As part of all this, I have to be really visible, so I go out and I police lots of matches – around four or five a week – from club matches to England games. You're embedded in football and at the clubs. It's a really varied role and very interesting.

It sounds it. How did you get into it?

I didn't grow up wanting to be a police officer. I had a bit of a boring job after university and a friend who had joined the police inspired me to change careers. I joined without any expectations, but I never looked back. It quickly became obvious I like adrenaline-filled situations. Things like riot policing – so you've got the big helmet on, and all the kit. That's really my area.

Do you need to like football to do your job?

Yes. And you have to understand what's going on in the game. If I needed to speak to the fans and I knew nothing about football, I'd have zero credibility. But when I talk about what the squad's like, or who I think should be playing, or how long someone's been out injured, that brings me a massive amount of credibility with the people I deal with.

Do the fans get to know and trust you?

I hope so. I know there are some supporters I see week in, week out who aren't troublemakers, but at one game someone might say something to them that riles them, and I will calm that situation down. Because they know that if I say, 'Leave that with me,' I will sort it. They have that trust and confidence in me. People know that if I do end up going in and arresting somebody, I am fair and I'm doing it in the right way.

PROUDEST MOMENTS

There have been some amazing opportunities when working on England matches. I went to the World Cup in Qatar in 2022, and I did the European Championship Final at Wembley. That was probably the pinnacle, albeit a very challenging one.

We did a documentary with Rio Ferdinand because we were involved in a case where he was racially abused, and he thanked us and the team personally.

Four years ago, I pitched the idea of having a dedicated Football Hate Crime Officer, and everyone said we didn't need it. But, nationally, there are now about five or six. I'm one of those individuals who tries to drive change, and some of the groundbreaking work we've done in hate crime has been really important.

What are the downsides?

You do get a lot of abuse – not everybody likes the police, and there is an element of risk to your role. It's long hours, it's hard work, it's not very glamorous. You aren't always going to be popular, but you keep people safe.

What would you say to a young girl reading this, who is thinking about being a police officer?

This is not a gender-specific job, it's about character. If you're the sort of person who has confidence, wants to do the right thing and stands by their beliefs, then your gender is irrelevant. There's a place for everybody.

Could it be YOU?

Skills Lizzie would look for in a potential football police officer are:

- **Interested in football**
- **Someone who talks to people and builds a connection with them**
- **Someone alert to problems around them, who can notice a change in atmosphere**
- **A peacemaker**
- **The person who steps in when a situation kicks off to calm things down**

LIZZIE SAYS:
'If your local police force runs a cadet scheme, that's a really good place to start . . .'

FOOTBALL AUTHOR

Dan Freedman

Do you ever daydream about football? Imagine turning those daydreams into your job . . .

46

FOOTBALL AUTHOR

DAN FREEDMAN

'I LIVE OUT MY FOOTBALL DREAMS THROUGH THE CHARACTERS IN MY STORIES.'

- Has sold over a million books around the world
- One of the authors of this book!
- Wrote the *Jamie Johnson* series
- Has interviewed both Ronaldo and Messi!

INTERVIEW

What does an author do?

I write stories and if they're good enough, a publisher will turn them into books for people around the world to read.

Are all your books about football?

It's definitely been a consistent theme because there's so much drama, passion and action in the game. And also because of the way it brings people together. That's how I got into football in the first place – I didn't live with my dad, but we went to watch football together.

Were you a good writer at school?

I actually didn't have much confidence in my writing at school. I didn't think I had a great imagination. But I had one good teacher who believed in me and, over time, I understood that stories can be about anything, including the things you're most passionate about – like football.

Have you had a pinch-me moment?

Jude Bellingham saying that he grew up watching the *Jamie Johnson* TV series and almost feels like he is Jamie Johnson now!

What was your big break?

Working with the England team for seven years. I was the in-house journalist, so it was my job to report on all the games and interview the players. Those experiences were a huge inspiration for the stories I went on to write. I was lucky enough to travel and work with players like Beckham, Rooney and Gerrard. I just had so many football stories in my head. That's where the *Jamie Johnson* series came from. Jamie was a mixture of those players and my own experiences growing up.

What did you ask Messi when you interviewed him?

Ha ha – I said: 'What does it feel like to be the greatest player on the planet?'

He said that all he thinks about each day is just how he can get better. Scary thought for defenders!

Have any players read your books?

Yes! One of the best was when Marcus Rashford read my sporty thriller *Unstoppable*. He said it reminded him of his household when he was growing up and then he posted on social media about it too!

Could YOU do it?

If you'd like to write a football story that gets turned into a book, here are Dan's top tips:

- ⚽ Use your own life experiences in your writing. It will give you confidence and also make your story unique.

- ⚽ Really get to know your characters. Ask them lots of questions: what's their favourite pizza? What's their middle name? What's their biggest fear? Once you understand them, it will feel like they're writing the story for you.

- ⚽ Don't expect your first try to be perfect. Writing is a process. Start by putting something down on paper, then have a look and see what you can improve. Then just keep going along like that.

⚽ Plan what happens. Some writers just sit down and see where the story takes them. I'm not that good! I need a plan. In my mind, I often see the end of the story first, then it's a case of making sure the rest of the story builds towards that moment.

⚽ Don't be afraid to change tactics. Even if you do have a plan, don't be afraid to change it if you come up with a better idea along the way.

⚽ Make the reader care. The most important element of a really good story is when the reader cares about what's happening to the characters. So, how do we make the reader care? Try giving your main character a goal and then put lots of challenges in the way. That way, the reader will be supporting the character along the way.

⚽ Rejection is part of the game. My first novel was rejected by every publisher for three years, so don't worry if the same thing happens to you. It'll make it even sweeter when you finally succeed!

●● FIND IT ONLINE! ✖

Search: 'Skills From Brazil – 1st Chapter read by Dan Freedman' to watch Dan reading from one of his favourite *Jamie Johnson* novels.

LET'S GO

DOCUMENTARY MAKER
Ben Turner

Imagine making a documentary about the team you love or the greatest players to have ever lived. Ben Turner has done exactly that. He takes you behind the scenes of his life in TV . . .

47

DOCUMENTARY MAKER

BEN TURNER

Made the Netflix documentary Sunderland 'Til I Die

Made *Captains of the World*, filming Messi winning the World Cup!

Has directed music videos for Harry Styles and Little Mix

'FIND SOMETHING THAT YOU'RE OBSESSED BY. IT GIVES YOU A SUPERPOWER.'

INTERVIEW

How did you know you wanted to be a documentary maker?

As a kid, there was a video that my brother and I kept watching, which told the stories of the World Cups from 1966 to 1986. We LOVED watching it. I didn't realise it at the time, but I think that's what planted the seed.

How did you realise you could do it?

The first time I ever did video editing, I thought, *Oh my gosh, I really get this, and I really know how to do this.*

Editing is the point where you take all the stuff you've filmed and put it together into a story. You decide which shots you're going to cut, which ones you're going to use and how long they're going to be on screen. You basically make the film in the edit. I knew straight away that was what I was supposed to do.

I don't like being the focus of attention, with everyone looking at me. As a film-maker, you find someone else to do that job for you – but you get to craft the story, and I love that.

What was your big break?

My brother, my friends and I made a film together called *In the Hands of the Gods*. We did it ourselves and that was a real game-changer because when you're trying to get into any industry, the question is: what have you done already? It's really tricky, as you need money to fund these projects in the first place. Fortunately, we had that little chance and it kind of flew, so that opened the doors for us.

Which documentary are you most proud of?

I think *Sunderland 'Til I Die* (Netflix). I'm very proud of many things, but the biggest constant in my life has been my love of Sunderland Football Club.

This documentary taps into something that other football fans can really connect with. It's very special for me.

Have you had a pinch-me moment?

Spending time with the Brazilian Ronaldo. He is the greatest: everyone who knows him, whenever you mention him, they just smile.

Things will always go wrong. In my first few productions when things started to go wrong, I felt it was a massive failure. Now when things go wrong, I'm focused on how to fix it rather than beating myself up about it. You need to be comfortable with failing – it's how you succeed.

GETTING THERE

Here's Ben's advice for those who want to follow in his footsteps . . .

 If you're waiting for someone to give you the go-ahead, it's not going to happen. Start making stuff on your phone or on a camera, and then you can show it to people (which will impress them). Begin to learn your craft and keep developing your voice.

 You have to start straight away, because you've got lots to learn. Your first film won't be perfect. It will be rubbish – and that's OK. The second thing you do will be a tiny bit less rubbish, and that's OK. And then you will keep getting less and less rubbish, until you start getting good. But if you don't keep working through the rubbish phase then you'll be stuck there forever. If you start now, when your opportunity comes, you'll be ready.

Kaammini Chanrai

Brentford FC

'Football is for everyone' is a phrase we hear a lot. For Kaammini Chanrai, it's her job . . .

KAAMMINI CHANRAI

47

48 EQUALITY, DIVERSITY AND INCLUSION DIRECTOR

DOCUMENT...

Studied gender, development and globalisation

Previously worked in inclusion at Warner Bros, Discovery and Vodafone

Is a trustee for Agenda, the alliance for women and girls at risk

'YOU MIGHT BE FROM THE LGBTQ+ COMMUNITY, WATCHING AT HOME. YOU SEE A RAINBOW FLAG IN OUR STADIUM. THAT'S A HUGE MESSAGE WE'RE SENDING OUT TO SAY, "WE'RE WITH YOU, WE SUPPORT YOU."'

WE'RE WITH YOU, WE SUPPORT YOU

INTERVIEW

Can you explain what you do?

My job is to make sure that everyone who interacts with the club in any way, whether that's staff, players, fans or the local community, really feels that Brentford is a place where they can belong, feel safe, feel valued and be treated fairly.

I listen to people to understand their needs on how we can better support them and then act on those conversations. That might involve putting education in place for people, physically making changes to our stadium or our working environment, or celebrating different communities and running campaigns. I also want to make sure that everybody employed at Brentford understands the importance of equity, diversity and inclusion, and is working towards that common goal, because it matters to us as a club.

Why is this job important for you?

Being a woman from an ethnic minority background, I adored football but never thought it was for me. I would hate to think that the game is missing out on all these incredible, amazing people from across the world who feel that same way. That's why I'm personally very motivated to do the job I do. When Brentford approached me, I took one look at the job description and one look at the club's values, and I thought if there was ever going to be a club I would join, it would be this one.

How interested are the players and manager in what you do?

BeeTogether is one of our core values at Brentford and it's something that our manager Thomas Frank embodies. The players are also very passionate about it. Some, like Ivan Toney, have gone into schools to talk about equality and inclusion.

We also put on sessions for the players; for example, we ran one about Ramadan and how we can make sure we're supporting those who'll be fasting.

One of the most powerful sessions we've had was when we invited Dr Neville Lawrence to speak to the players. Dr Lawrence is the father of Stephen Lawrence, a Black teenager who was killed in a racist attack. That was hugely impactful because many of the players weren't born when Stephen Lawrence was murdered, but they resonated with a lot of what was said. We had really interesting discussions about allyship and how they can support one another as players in this wider conversation about race.

Could it be YOU?

Do you feel passionately about fairness and diversity in football? If so, then maybe you could follow in Kaammini's footsteps. Here's her advice:

- The number-one thing is a passion for wanting to make the world a better place. It sounds really cheesy, but that is the entry point.

- If you enjoy helping other kids at school fit in more, that's a great starting point, because that's what equity, diversity and inclusion is all about. It's about ensuring that people feel like they have friends and they belong. Different skills like communication and being good with data are useful, but really it's about wanting to help.

- History is a good subject to study at school because in order to know how we can create a better future, we need to understand and learn from the past.

- Wanting to know more about other people and celebrating their stories also goes to the heart of this job.

- If you're interested in events such as East and South East Asian Heritage Month, Black History Month, Jewish heritage and culture days, Pride, International Day of Persons with Disabilities, Windrush Day, International Men's Day and International Women's Day, then this might be an area you could work in. Everyone has a story, and sharing those stories is a big part of what we do.

HEAD OF PR

Tony Stevens

Tottenham Hotspur FC

Looking after a football club's reputation is a big responsibility. Tony Stevens gets to do it for the club he loves.

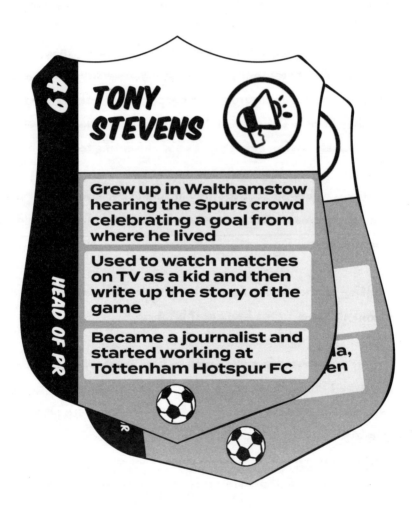

49

HEAD OF PR

TONY STEVENS

Grew up in Walthamstow hearing the Spurs crowd celebrating a goal from where he lived

Used to watch matches on TV as a kid and then write up the story of the game

Became a journalist and started working at Tottenham Hotspur FC

INTERVIEW

What does the head of PR do at a football club?

I promote the good work that the club does, away from football. Everyone knows about what Spurs do on the pitch, but there's so much more to a football club, especially one our size and as invested in its local community as we are.

I help to tell those stories via our own club channels, social media, newspapers, radio and TV, so that everyone who is interested in Spurs (which is about six hundred million people around the world) can know what we're doing as a club to impact people's lives in a positive way.

You must have been involved in telling some amazing stories?

There have been moments during my time at Spurs that will never leave me. Probably the most notable ones were when we left White Hart Lane and then opened the new stadium.

Opening the stadium wasn't just a moment in the club's history – it was a landmark occasion for Tottenham itself, an area which has had huge levels of social and economic deprivation and seen two riots in the last few decades.

We wanted the new stadium opening to be a turning point and invited the youth of Tottenham to sing the 'Song of Hope' in the ceremony. Five years on, and we're now starting to see that story play out in reality. The stadium is so much more than a football pitch. It's jobs for local people and a venue for international stars like Beyoncé to perform concerts!

Have you built a close relationship with any of the players?

Absolutely – I've done a lot of work with Ledley King and also with Jermain Defoe, who has become a good friend. He's very aware of the challenges of growing up in London. I also have to mention the chairman, Daniel Levy, because everything the club does, not only on the pitch but also in its ambitions to regenerate this area, is all part of his vision.

BIG BREAK!

I was working for a sports journalism agency called Hayters. I'd tried really hard to stand out and, after a year, they said to me, 'Do you want to follow Spurs on their pre-season tour?' It was in France and I was the only journalist out there, so that allowed me to get myself known around the club. A year later, I heard about a vacancy in Spurs' media department. I went for it and that's where my journey within the club began.

'THIS CLUB FEELS LIKE FAMILY TO ME AND TO HAVE PLAYED A SMALL PART IN ITS HISTORY FILLS ME WITH IMMENSE PRIDE.'

GETTING THERE

Tony's top tips for following in his footsteps

⚽ You've got to have an eye for a story.

⚽ How we communicate with people is key to what we do, so you need to have that belief in the power of the spoken and written word.

⚽ You need a good grasp of vocabulary and to be able to tell things simply – not just looking at how you see them, but also being able to think about how someone looking from the outside would view them.

⚽ It's also about having an interest in news and current affairs, whether in the context of sports or wider events. Football doesn't operate in isolation; it's interconnected with what's happening in the world.

⚽ More broadly, don't be afraid of hard work, long hours and taking on new things outside of your comfort zone.

⚽ Remember that everyone you come across can teach you something, so be willing to learn from them.

⚽ Stay in contact with people, because every person you meet could be the person that changes your life one day.

● ● ○ FIND IT ONLINE! ✖

Search: 'Tottenham Hotspur Stadium Opening Ceremony' to see the event that Tony and his team put together for this historic occasion.

LET'S GO

PE TEACHER
Caroline Bolton

If you love sport and want to help young people learn about it, improve their physical fitness and get into different sports, becoming a PE teacher could be the job for you. We spoke to Caroline Bolton, who does exactly that.

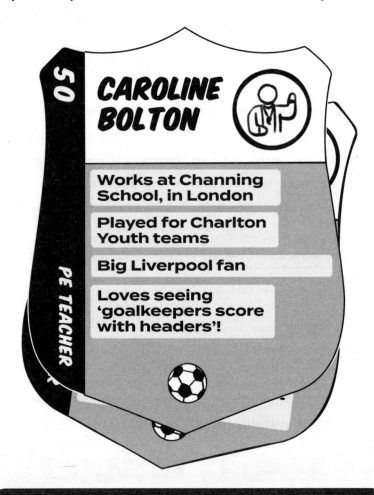

50

PE TEACHER

CAROLINE BOLTON

- Works at Channing School, in London
- Played for Charlton Youth teams
- Big Liverpool fan
- Loves seeing 'goalkeepers score with headers'!

'YOU NEVER LOSE, YOU ALWAYS LEARN.'

INTERVIEW

How did you get into football and were you a good player?

I had tried every other sport, but I just couldn't stick with them for longer than three weeks. Then my cousin joined a football club and it looked really good, so I joined too.

At primary school, I was one of only three girls in our football team. We'd turn up at tournaments and people would look at us and ask, 'What's this?' And, actually, we were better than half the boys that we were playing.

I tell the girls I teach at school that if they ever play against boys, it's going to be hard because the boys don't want to be shown up by girls.

When did you think you might want to work in football?

When I left school, I didn't really know what I wanted to be. I just knew I didn't want to be stuck in an office – I wanted to be out and about, doing a practical job, so I almost signed up for a plumbing apprenticeship. I was playing for Charlton but in those days, you couldn't make enough money to have it as your job. So I thought that if I couldn't play, I'd do something else in the game. I got some work experience in a local primary school, teaching PE, and I loved it.

I just liked being able to excite the children. I felt like I was making an impact because everyone was having a great time.

What's being a PE teacher like?

You're on your feet, running around, trying to be inspirational and motivational, so you need lots of energy, patience and passion. Also, you're doing a range of different sports, not just football. We start before school, with pre-lesson activities, and then our timetable is jam-packed. Some days you might have a fixture during the afternoon and then we have after-school clubs too, so it's just busy all the time!

What's the best part of the job?

Inspiring the next generation. My proudest moment was when the football squad won the Haringey tournament. It was the start of something special.

COULD YOU DO IT?

As a PE teacher, it'll be your job to select teams for competitions, which also means explaining your decision to players who haven't made it. Could you do that?

Have YOU got the SKILLS?

These are some of the key skills you'll need if you want to be a good PE teacher:

Good sporting ability

Leadership and decision making skill

Top communication

Knowledge of the human body

Ability to motivate and inspire young people

Able to organise and think on your feet

Remain calm and show empathy

INSPIRATIONAL TEACHER

Like Caroline, there are lots of teachers who have inspired their pupils to pursue careers in football. Ex-footballer Ian Wright was encouraged to pursue football by his teacher Mr Pigden. Watch their emotional reunion on YouTube. It's a tear-jerker!

Who's your favourite teacher? How do they inspire you?

AUTHORS

DAN FREEDMAN

Dan Freedman dreamed of being a professional footballer. That didn't happen. When he was thirteen, his mum said: 'Why don't you try to be a football writer instead?'

And so he did, first becoming a journalist with the England national team and then writing the *Jamie Johnson* series of novels.

He's sold over a million books around the world and visited more than two thousand schools to encourage young people to go for their goals, on and off the pitch.

DANIEL GEEY

Daniel Geey was lucky enough to grow up going with his dad, brother and family to watch Liverpool at Anfield. He became obsessed with the goals, transfer gossip and Championship Manager.

Lots of his family members were lawyers so he thought he better study law at university too. He became a lawyer and after a while started working with players, agents and clubs. He's written two books, 250+ blogs and is the host of *The Daniel Geey Podcast*.

Dan and Daniel teamed up for *50 Ways Into Football*, their first book together.

Hopefully the first of many.

ACKNOWLEDGEMENTS

We are indebted to all the wonderful contributors to this book for sharing their time and expertise. And to:

David Luxton for his guidance, wisdom and support in turning the idea into a reality. Helen Archer, Laura Horsley, Anna Martin, Pippi Grantham-Wright, Emily Thomas, Antara Bate and the wonderful team at Hachette for believing in us and producing this beautiful book.

Hollie, Issie and Liv Geey, for all your love, support and encouragement.

Sarah Martin, Louisa Botha and Tom Anderson for going above and beyond throughout the project.

Declan, Sean and Steph Rice for sharing your incredible journey.

And to all the people behind the scenes without whose help this book would not have been possible:

Wildey, Connor Rice, Luca Russo, Lola Cashman, Stuart Mawhinney, Paul Boanas, Hilary Messenger, Mark Whittle, Joanne Whittle, Matt Kleinman, Ian Cruise, George Baldwin, Luca Russo, James Marshall, Steve Fletcher, Katie Holmes, Greg Demetriou, Felicity Still, Danny Lynch, Kieran Owen, Chloe Reid, Georgia Hefferman, Owen O'Donnell, Tony Hamilton, Gillian Gallacher, Martin Prothero, Megan Rumsey, Ben Campbell, Max Fitzgerald, Matt Vines, Richard Cox, Nikita Rathod, Paul Sampson, Alex Othol, Fred Chesher, Jo Bartlett, Caroline Rudoni, Simon Humphrey, Andrew Sinclair, Ant Farley.

IF YOU LIKE THIS BOOK, WHY NOT TRY . . .

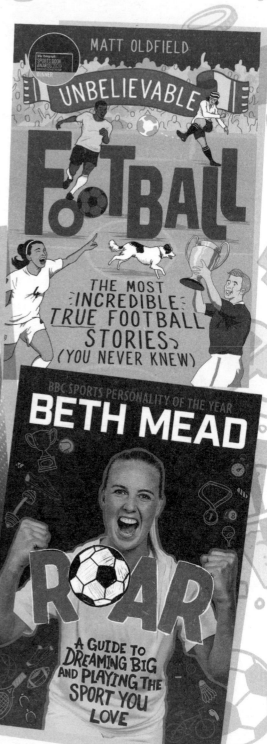

MATT OLDFIELD

UNBELIEVABLE FOOTBALL

THE MOST INCREDIBLE TRUE FOOTBALL STORIES (YOU NEVER KNEW)

EVE AINSWORTH
Illustrated by Dan Leydon

KELLY

SCOTT

GAME CHANGERS

WOMEN'S FOOTBALL
THE HISTORY, THE STARS, THE STATS AND THE GOALS!

BBC SPORTS PERSONALITY OF THE YEAR
BETH MEAD

ROAR

A GUIDE TO DREAMING BIG AND PLAYING THE SPORT YOU LOVE